Renaissance & Reformation
Primary Sources

Renaissance & Reformation
Primary Sources

PEGGY SAARI &
AARON SAARI, EDITORS

Julie Carnagie, Project Editor

THOMSON

GALE

Detroit • New York • San Diego • San Francisco • Cleveland • New Haven, Conn. • Waterville, Maine • London • Munich

THOMSON
GALE

Renaissance and Reformation: Primary Sources

Peggy Saari and Aaron Saari

Project Editor
Julie L. Carnagie

Permissions
Shalice Shah-Caldwell

Imaging and Multimedia
Robert Duncan, Kelly A. Quin

Product Design
Pamela A. Galbreath

Composition
Evi Seoud

Manufacturing
Rita Wimberly

LIBRARY OF CONGRESS CATALOGING-IN-PUBLICATION DATA

Renaissance and Reformation : primary sources / [compiled by] Peggy Saari and Aaron Saari; Julie L. Carnagie, editor.

p. cm.

Includes bibliographical references and index.

ISBN 0-7876-5473-6 (Hardcover : alk. paper)

1. Renaissance–Sources–Juvenile literature. 2. Reformation–Sources–Juvenile literature. [1. Renaissance–Sources. 2. Reformation–Sources.] I. Saari, Peggy. II. Saari, Aaron Maurice. III. Carnagie, Julie.

CB359 .R465 2002

940.2–dc21

2002003928

Contents

Reader's Guide

Renaissance and Reformation: Primary Sources presents eighteen full or excerpted documents written by people who lived during the Renaissance and Reformation period. The autobiographical essays, diary entries, poems, trial testimonies, and letters in this volume reflect the experiences of religious reformers, world leaders, early scientists, authors, and artists. Some entries such as William Shakespeare's *The Merchant of Venice* and Miguel de Cervantes's *Don Quixote* display just some of the extensive literature and drama that was being written during the Renaissance period. Other excerpts, including Martin Luther's "The Ninety-Five Theses" and Teresa de Ávila's *The Life of Teresa of Jesus,* are meant to detail the causes of the Protestant Reformation and the experiences of people living through the Catholic Reformation.

Format

Renaissance and Reformation: Primary Sources is divided into six chapters. Each chapter focuses on a specific theme: Humanism, Renaissance Arts and Science, Drama and Literature, Protestant Reformation, Catholic Reformation, and Witch-hunts. All of the chapters open with a historical overview, followed by the appropriate primary source documents.

Each excerpt is divided into six sections:

- **Introductory material** places the document and its author in a historical context

- **Things to remember** offers readers important background information about the featured text

- **Excerpt** presents the document in its original format

- **What happened next** discusses the impact of the document on both the speaker and his or her audience

- **Did you know** provides interesting facts about each document and its author

- **For more information** presents sources for more information on documents and speakers

Additional Features

Many of the *Renaissance and Reformation: Primary Sources* contain sidebar boxes examining related excerpts, events, and issues, while more than forty black-and-white photos help illustrate the text. Each excerpt is accompanied by a glossary running alongside the primary document that defines terms, people, and ideas discussed within each document. Also included within the volume is a timeline of important events and a subject index of the topics discussed in *Renaissance and Reformation: Primary Sources*.

Comments and suggestions

We welcome your comments on this work as well as your suggestions for topics to be featured in future editions of *Renaissance and Reformation: Primary Sources*. Please write: Editors, *Renaissance and Reformation: Primary Sources*, U•X•L, 27500 Drake Rd., Farmington Hills, MI 48331-3535; call toll-free: 1-800-877-4253; fax: 248-699-8097; or send e-mail via www.gale.com.

Timeline of Events

1377 Arab scholar **Ibn Khaldún** completes *The Muqaddimah,* now regarded as one of the greatest masterpieces of all time. The work represents a significant leap forward in scholarship since it attempts to describe patterns in social and political organizations.

1451 **Isotta Nogarola** writes "On the Equal and Unequal Sin of Eve and Adam," which is considered the first piece of feminist writing.

1458 **Margaret of Navarre**'s *Heptaméron* is published and becomes an important work of the Renaissance period.

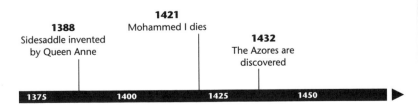

1388
Sidesaddle invented by Queen Anne

1421
Mohammed I dies

1432
The Azores are discovered

| 1375 | 1400 | 1425 | 1450 |

1486 Austrian priest **Heinrich Kramer** and German priest **James Sprenger** publish *Malleus Maleficarum,* which becomes the official handbook for detecting, capturing, trying, and executing witches.

1490s Italian painter, sculptor, engineer, and scientist **Leonardo da Vinci** begins keeping notebooks in which he records his ideas on a wide range of topics. He also illustrates the notebooks with drawings that demonstrate his concepts.

1513 Italian diplomat **Niccolò Machiavelli** writes *The Prince,* in which he explains his controversial political philosophy: a ruler must be motivated solely by self-interest and must place the survival of his regime above all other considerations.

1517 German priest **Martin Luther** posts "Ninety-Five Theses" in response to the Catholic Church's misuse of the sale of indulgences.

1523 Swiss priest **Huldrych Zwingli** issues "Sixty-Seven Articles," which offered solutions to major problems in the church and becomes an outline for religious reform in Zurich.

1536 French-born Protestant reformer **John Calvin** writes the first edition of *Institutes of the Christian Religion.* In this work Calvin states that the all-knowing and ever-present God had determined, from the beginning of time, who was to be saved and who was to be damned.

1548 Spanish priest **Ignatius of Loyola** publishes *Spiritual Exercises.* The work becomes highly influential with the church, and its exercises continue to be followed by Catholics today.

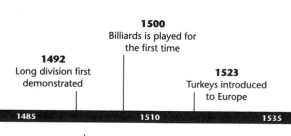

1500
Billiards is played for the first time

1492
Long division first demonstrated

1523
Turkeys introduced to Europe

1485   1510   1535   1560

1564 Pope Pius IV releases the "Profession of the Tridentine Faith," which is a summary of the major decisions reached by the Council of Trent regarding reforms within the **Roman Catholic Church.**

1573 Dutch Anabaptist **Elizabeth** writes "Elizabeth, A Dutch Anabaptist martyr: A letter" shortly before she is executed. The letter was written to Elizabeth's daughter Janneken as a guide for her moral and spiritual development.

1580 French author **Michel de Montaigne** publishes *Essays,* containing the piece titled "Of Cannibals." This essay draws comparisons between supposedly "civilized" French society and so-called "barbarians."

1596 English playwright **William Shakespeare**'s best-known comedy, *Merchant of Venice,* is first performed.

1605 **Miguel de Cervantes** publishes the first part of *Don Quixote,* considered one of the great masterpieces of world literature.

1610 Italian astronomer **Galileo Galilei** publishes *Starry Messenger.* The booklet, which presents many of Galileo's sensational discoveries, takes the world of science by storm.

1611 *The Life of Teresa of Jesus* is published. It is the autobiography of **Teresa de Ávila,** a religious mystic and founder of the Reformed Discalced Carmelite order.

1666 English author **Margaret Cavendish** publishes *The Description of a New World Called the Blazing World,* which is often called one of the first science fiction novels.

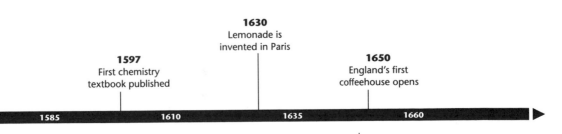

1630
Lemonade is
invented in Paris

1597
First chemistry
textbook published

1650
England's first
coffeehouse opens

1585   1610   1635   1660

Humanism

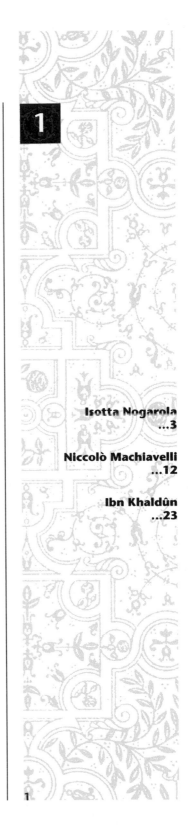

The Renaissance produced an explosion of written works—translations of ancient texts, scholarly studies, biblical interpretations, histories, philosophical treatises, scientific theories, religious pamphlets, biographies, social commentaries, poetry, stories, novels, and plays, to name but a few. Many factors contributed to this development, but there were two major influences: the humanist movement and the invention of the printing press. The humanist movement began in Italy in the mid-1300s as a revival of the literature and culture of ancient Greece and Rome, which focused on human experience and creativity. Within a few decades scholars and thinkers throughout Europe were promoting a human-centered view of the world. Italian humanists are credited with founding the Renaissance, which was given momentum a century later, in the mid-1400s, by the printing press. Written works could be mass-produced and quickly distributed throughout Europe. Thus Renaissance ideals spread rapidly, leading to new ways of observing and writing about every aspect of human endeavor.

During the fifteenth century the humanist movement inspired the study of ancient Greek and Roman texts as well as new interpretations of the Bible. A unique biblical interpretation was written by the Italian scholar Isotta Nogarola, the first prominent woman humanist. In "On the Equal or Unequal Sin of Adam and Eve" she examined the Garden of Eden story in the Old Testament from the perspective of Eve. This is considered the first feminist reading of the story. As humanism gained momentum in the early1500s, scholars turned their attention to European history and politics. A classic work from this era is *The Prince,* in which the Italian diplomat Niccolò Machiavelli described the qualities of the ideal ruler and defined politics as a separate field of philosophy.

A few decades after humanism began evolving in Italy in the fourteenth century, the Arab scholar Ibn Khaldûn completed *The Muqaddimah,* the introduction to his history of the world. Like the European humanists, Ibn Khaldûn used ancient Greek concepts to examine society from ancient times to his own day in *The Muqaddimah.* This work is now regarded as the basis of modern sociology.

Isotta Nogarola

Excerpt from "On the Equal or Unequal Sin of Eve and Adam" (1451)

Reprinted in *Her Immaculate Hand: Selected Works By and About The Women Humanists of Quattrocento Italy*

**Edited and translated by Margaret L. King and Albert Rabil Jr.
Published in 1983**

The Italian scholar Isotta Nogarola (1418–1466) is considered the first major female humanist. "Humanism" is the modern term for the intellectual movement that initiated the Renaissance. The humanist movement originated in Florence, Italy, in the mid-1300s and was introduced into other European countries shortly before 1500. Humanist scholars believed that a body of learning called *studia humanitatis* (humanistic studies), which was based on the literary masterpieces from the classical period of ancient Greece and Rome, could bring about a cultural rebirth, or renaissance. The texts included not only classical literature but also the Bible (the Christian holy book) and the works of early Christian thinkers. Humanists were committed to the revival of ancient works as a way to end the "barbarism" (lack of refinement or culture) of the Middle Ages (also called the medieval period), the thousand-year era that followed the downfall of the Roman Empire in the fourth and fifth centuries. Humanistic studies were nearly always developed with the education of boys and the careers of men in mind. Nonetheless, a few educators promoted classical education for women.

During the fifteenth century humanism spread rapidly from Florence to the elite social classes in other Italian cities, such as Venice, Padua, Verona, Bologna, Milan, and Genoa, then extended south to Rome and Naples. Many scholars, writers, intellectuals, and patrons contributed to the development of humanism. Women were active in the earliest stages of the movement, which created an environment for the free expression of their ideas. The first to emerge was Isotta Nogarola. Born into a literary family in Verona, she received a humanist education along with her sister Ginevra. During an intellectual career that spanned more than thirty years, Isotta wrote Latin prose and poetry and participated in learned conferences and debates. She is most famous for her extensive correspondence with humanist friends. These letters demonstrate Nogarola's knowledge of early Christian and classical authors, as well as her awareness of current political events and the historical tradition of heroic women. The letters also show that she had close relationships with the intellectual and political leaders of northern Italy. Many of the people who corresponded with Nogarola showered her with praise, suggesting that she was widely known for exceptional achievements.

Among Nogarola's admirers were leading humanists in Venice, Lauro Quirini and Ludovico Foscarini. Quirini outlined a program of study that urged Nogarola to reach beyond literature written in Latin to read philosophical works in the original Greek. He argued that Greek philosophy (the search for an understanding of reality through speculation) is superior to Roman rhetoric (the art of effective speaking and writing). He suggested that a learned woman had the capacity to master the difficulties of philosophy. Of special interest is the letter exchange between Nogarola and the Italian humanist Ludovico Foscarini, who was a Venetian statesman and governor of Verona. In 1451 Nogarola composed a dialogue (written work in the form of a conversation) titled "On the Equal or Unequal Sin of Eve and Adam." It is a debate between herself and Foscarini on the question of whether Eve had committed a greater sin than Adam in the Garden of Eden. This is Nogarola's best-known work.

Things to Remember While Reading an Excerpt from "On the Equal or Unequal Sin of Eve and Adam":

- "On the Equal or Unequal Sin of Eve and Adam" was written entirely by Nogarola. She composed the dialogue, with Foscarini's encouragement, from letters she and Foscarini had exchanged on the subject of Adam and Eve.

- According to the story in the book of Genesis in the Old Testament (the first part of the Bible), Adam and Eve were the first two people on Earth. They lived in the Garden of Eden, a perfect world, and they had no awareness of evil because they had been forbidden by God to eat apples from the tree of knowledge in the garden. One day an evil serpent, or snake, appeared in the tree and tempted Adam and Eve to eat an apple. Eve took a bite from the apple and then persuaded Adam to do the same. God later expelled them from the garden for disobeying his command and committing the first sin. Nogarola quotes extensively from the book of Genesis in "On the Equal or Unequal Sin of Eve and Adam."

- The Adam and Eve story was used first by Jewish prophets, or wise men, and later by Christian thinkers to prove that Eve was responsible for the fact that all humans are born with original sin. That is, sin is a part of human nature from birth because Eve (woman) had tempted Adam (man) into an awareness of evil.

- In "On the Equal or Unequal Sin of Eve and Adam" Foscarini takes Adam's side on the question of who had committed the greater sin. Thus he presents the traditional argument for Eve's guilt. He points out that Eve's moral weakness, not the serpent, or evil, was the temptation that made Adam surrender to a sinful act.

- Nogarola defends Eve, saying that Eve "had less intellect" than Adam and therefore was incapable of choosing between good and evil. For this reason, Nogarola argues, Eve should not be held responsible for original sin.

- The following excerpts from "On the Equal or Unequal Sin of Eve and Adam" represent only a portion of the lengthy and complex debate between Nogarola and Foscarini. The dialogue is typical of philosophical works written in this form on a wide variety of topics by humanists during the Renaissance.

Excerpts from
"On the Equal or Unequal Sin of Eve and Adam"

*Ludovico begins: If it is in any way possible to measure the **gravity** of human sinfulness, then we should see Eve's sin as more to be condemned than Adam's [for three reasons]. [First], she was assigned by a **just judge** to a harsher punishment than was Adam. [Second], she believed that she was made more like God, and that is in the category of unforgivable sins against the **Holy Spirit**. [Third], she suggested and was the cause of Adam's sin—not he of hers; and although it is a poor excuse to sin because of a friend, nevertheless none was more tolerable than the one by which Adam was enticed.*

*Isotta: But I see things—since you move me to reply—from quite another and contrary viewpoint. For where there is less intellect and less **constancy,** there is less sin; and Eve [lacked sense and constancy] and therefore sinned less. Knowing [her weakness] that crafty serpent began by tempting the woman, thinking the man perhaps **invulnerable** because of his constancy....*

*[Adam must also be judged more guilty then Eve, secondly] because of his greater contempt for the command. For in Genesis 2 it appears that the Lord commanded Adam, not Eve, where it says: "The Lord God took the man and placed him in the paradise of Eden to **till** it and keep it," (and it does not say, "that they might care for and protect it") "... and the Lord God commanded the man" (and not "them"): "From every tree of the garden you may eat" (and not "you" [in the plural sense]), and, [referring to the forbidden tree], "for the day you eat of it, you must die," [again, using the singular form of "you"]. [God directed his command to Adam alone] because he esteemed the man more highly than the woman.*

Moreover, the woman did not [eat from the forbidden tree] because she believed that she was made more like God, but rather because she was weak and [inclined to indulge in] pleasure. Thus: "Now the woman saw that the tree was good for food, pleasing to the eyes, and desirable for the knowledge it would give. She

Gravity: Seriousness.

Just judge: God.

Holy Spirit: The third person of the Christian Trinity (God the Father, Son, and Holy Spirit).

Constancy: Fidelity, loyalty.

Invulnerable: Incapable of being wounded, injured, or harmed.

Till: Work soil by plowing, planting, and raising crops.

Christ: Name for Jesus of Nazareth, founder of Christianity.

Incarnate: In bodily form.

Posterity: Future generations.

Perdition: Loss of the soul.

Synagogue: Jewish house of worship.

Purged: To become rid of sin.

took of its fruit and ate it, and also gave some to her husband and he ate," and it does not say *[that she did so]* in order to be like God. And if Adam had not eaten, her sin would have had no consequences. For it does not say: "If Eve had not sinned **Christ** would not have been made **incarnate**," but "If Adam had not sinned." Hence the woman, but only because she had been first deceived by the serpent's evil persuasion, did indulge in the delights of paradise; but she would have harmed only herself and in no way endangered human **posterity** if the consent of the first-born man had not been offered. Therefore Eve was no danger to posterity but [only] to herself; but the man Adam spread the infection of sin to himself and to all future generations. Thus Adam, being the author of all humans yet to be born, was also the first cause of their **perdition.** For this reason the healing of humankind was celebrated first in the man and then in the woman, just as [according to Jewish tradition], after the unclean spirit has been expelled from a man, as it springs forth from the **synagogue,** the woman is **purged** [as well].*

A painting of Adam and Eve, the biblical characters described in the book of Genesis. Isotta Nogarola's "On the Equal or Unequal Sin of Eve and Adam" set the stage for a later feminist rethinking of the Adam and Eve story. *Reproduced by permission of Hulton Archive.*

*Moreover, that Eve was condemned by a just judge to a harsher punishment is evidently false, for God said to the woman: "I will make great your distress in childbearing; in pain shall you bring forth children; for your husband shall be your longing, though he have dominion over you." But to Adam he said: "Because you have listened to your wife and have eaten of the tree of which I have commanded you not to eat" (notice that God appears to have **admonished** Adam alone [using the singular form of "you"] and not Eve) "Cursed be the ground because of you; in toil shall you eat of it all the days of your life; thorns and thistles shall it bring forth to you, and you shall eat the plants of the field. In the sweat of your brow you shall eat bread, till you return to the ground, since out of it you were taken; for dust you are and unto dust you shall return." Notice that Adam's punishment appears harsher than Eve's; for God said to Adam: "to dust you shall return," and not to Eve, and death is the most terrible punishment that could be assigned. Therefore it is established that Adam's punishment was greater then Eve's....*

*When God created man, from the beginning he created him perfect, and the powers of his soul perfect, and gave him a greater understanding and knowledge of truth as well as a greater depth of wisdom. Thus it was that the Lord led to Adam all the animals of the earth and the birds of heaven, so that Adam could call them by their names. For God said: "Let us make mankind in our image and likeness, and let them have dominion over the fish of the sea, and the birds of the air, the cattle, over all the wild animals and every creature that crawls on the earth," making clear his own perfection. But of the woman he said: "It is not good that the man is alone; I will make him a helper like himself." And since **consolation** and joy are required for happiness, and since no one can have **solace** and joy when alone, it appears that God created woman for man's consolation. For the good spreads itself, and the greater it is the more it shares itself. Therefore, it appears that Adam's sin was greater than Eve's....*

*Adam either had **free will** or he did not. If he did not have it, he did not sin; if he had it, then Eve forced the sin [upon him], which is impossible. . . . God could himself, however, remove that condition of liberty from any person and bestow some other condition on him. In the same way fire cannot, while it remains fire, not burn, unless its nature is changed and suspended for a time by divine force. No other creature, such as a good angel or devil can do this, since they are less than God; much less a woman, since she is less perfect and weaker then they.... Thus Adam appeared to accuse God rather than*

Admonished: Warned.

Consolation: Comfort.

Solace: Source of relief.

Free will: The power to make one's own choices.

excuse himself when he said: "The woman you placed at my side gave me fruit from the tree and I ate it."

Let these words be enough from me, an unarmed and poor little woman.

Ludovico: So divinely have you encompassed the whole of this problem that I could believe your words were drawn not from the **fonts** of philosophy and theology but from heaven. Hence they are worthy of praise rather than contradiction. Yet, lest you be cheated of the utility [you say you have begun to receive from this debate], attend to these brief arguments which can be posed for the opposite view, that you may sow the honey-sweet seeds of paradise which will delight readers and surround you with glory.

Eve's ignorance was very base, because she chose to put faith in a demon rather than in the creator. This ignorance actually is due to her sin, as sacred writings attest, and certainly does not excuse her of sin. Indeed, if the truth be plainly told, it was extreme stupidity to remain within the boundaries which the excellent God had set for her, [but] to fall **prey** to **vain** hope and lose what she had had and what she aspired to.

The issues which you have cleverly joined I shall not divide. The inconstancy of Eve which has been condemned was not inconstancy of nature but of habit. For those qualities which are in us by nature we are neither praised nor blamed, according to the judgement of the wisest philosophers. Actually, the woman's nature was excellent and **concordant** with reason, **genus** and time. For just as teeth were given to wild beasts, horns to oxen, feathers to birds for their survival, to the woman mental capacity was given sufficient for the preservation and pursuit of the health of her soul.

If [as you say] Eve was naturally created to aid, perfect, console and gladden man, she conducted herself contrary to the laws [of her nature], providing him with toil, imperfection, sadness and sorrow, which the holy decrees had ordained would be serious crimes. And human laws, too, ordered through long ages by the minds of great men, by sure reasoning have established that the seizure of someone else's goods merits the more serious punishment the more it injures the owner....

I have explained my views with these few words, both because I was ordered not to exceed the paper [you] sent me, and because I speak to you who are most learned. For I do not wish to be a guide on such a road to you for whom, because of your great goodness, all

Fonts: Sources; fountains.

Prey: Victim.

Vain: Useless.

Concordant: In agreement with.

Genus: Biological classification.

*things stand open in the brightest light. I, indeed—a single man and a mere mortal, as it were, a reflection of the **celestial** life—have only pointed a finger, so to speak, in the direction of the sources. And although others may find that my writings suffer from the defect of obscurity, if you, most brilliant, accept them and join them to what you and I have already written, our views will become very evident and clear, and will shine amid the shadows. And if what I have written is clumsy, by your skill you will make it worthy of your mind, virtue, and glory. For you march forward to new battles to the sound of sacred **eloquence** (as do soldiers to the **clamor** of trumpets), always more learned and more ready. And you march forward against me, who has applied the whole sum of my thinking to my reading, all at the same time, and to my writing, that I might present my case and defend myself against yours, although the many storms and floods of my obligation toss me about at **whim**. Farewell.*

What happened next...

At the time Foscarini was considered to be the winner of the debate because Nogarola had admitted that Eve was inferior to Adam in being unable to choose between right and wrong. Nevertheless, "On the Equal or Unequal Sin of Eve and Adam" set the stage for a later feminist rethinking of the Adam and Eve story. Nogarola produced a number of other works. Among them was a study of the early Christian father Saint Jerome (c. 347–419), which she wrote in 1453. Six years later she sent a letter to Pope Pius II (1405–1464; reigned 1458–64), urging him to start a crusade, or holy war. Nogarola's last five years were marked by illness. In 1468, two years after her death, the humanist Giovanni Mario Filelfo dedicated a lengthy poem to her brother, in which he celebrated her achievement as a holy woman. However, he omitted any mention of Isotta Nogarola's intellectual work.

Did you know...

• When Isotta Nogarola and her sister Ginevra were teenagers they attracted the attention of northern Italian

Celestial: Heavenly or divine.

Eloquence: Forceful or persuasive expressiveness.

Clamor: Insistent noise.

Whim: Sudden idea or turn of mind.

humanists and courtiers (members of noble courts). With these learned men Isotta and Ginevra exchanged books and letters that showed their classical training and lively intelligence. In 1438 Ginevra married and ceased her involvement in the discussions of humanist ideas.

- Isotta Nogarola continued to participate in humanist discussions until 1441, when she became discouraged by attacks on her character. Historians believe these attacks came from men who did not approve of learned women. Isotta Nogarola withdrew from humanist circles to join her mother in her brother's house. She lived, as she put it, in a "book-lined cell" where, like medieval holy women, she continued her studies in solitude.

- During the sixteenth and seventeenth centuries women became increasingly active in the humanist movement, which was given impetus by salons headed by women. A salon was an intellectual and literary discussion that became popular in the 1600s. Salons were instrumental in spreading new scientific and philosophical ideas and setting standards of literary taste. A salon was held at a royal or noble court and led by an aristocratic or high-born woman called a *salonnière*. The terms "salon" and *salonnière* were introduced in the nineteenth century. During the Renaissance salons were known as *ruelles* (companies). Many women who presided over and attended these gatherings exchanged ideas, then published their views in books and pamphlets.

For More Information

Book
King, Margaret L., and Albert Rabil Jr., eds. and trans. *Her Immaculate Hand: Selected Works By and About the Women Humanists of Quattrocento Italy.* Binghamton, N.Y.: Medieval and Renaissance Texts and Studies, 1983.

Web Sites
A Celebration of Women Writers: 1401–1500. [Online] Available http://digital.library.upenn.edu/women/_generate/1401-1500.html, April 10, 2002.

"Nogarola, Isotta." *Sunshine for Women.* [Online] Available http://www.pinn.net/~sunshine/march99/nogarla2.html, April 10, 2002.

Niccolò Machiavelli

Excerpts from **The Prince** *(1513)*
Reprinted in *The Renaissance Man*
Translated by Ninian Hill Thomson
Published in 1969

O ne of the most important works of the Renaissance was *The Prince* by the Italian author and statesman Niccolò Machiavelli (pronounced mahk-yah-VEL-lee;1469–1527). In this book Machiavelli explained his political philosophy, which remains controversial even today. According to Machiavelli, a ruler must be motivated solely by self-interest and must place the survival of his regime above all other considerations. Machiavelli developed his theories on the basis of humanist ideals. Humanism was a scholarly movement that began in Machiavelli's native city, Florence, Italy, in the mid-1300s. In the fifteenth and sixteenth centuries humanists set out to revive the culture of ancient Greece and Rome (called the classical period), which they considered the pinnacle of human achievement before the fall of the Roman Republic in the fourth and fifth centuries.

In the early 1500s humanists in Florence wanted to establish the city as the center of a resurrected Roman Republic. At that time France and Spain were involved in the early stages of a conflict over control of Italy, called the Italian Wars (1494–1559). Machiavelli saw the need for a strong political and military leader who could eliminate the French and Spanish presence in northern Italy by forming a unified state. He shared with Renaissance humanists a passion for classical antiquity. Though a republican (one who supports a government that represents the people) at heart, he had a fierce desire for political and moral renewal according to the ideals of the Roman Republic. When he wrote *The Prince* he envisioned such a possibility while the powerful Medicis family controlled Florence as well as the papacy in Rome. (The papacy is the office of the pope, who is the supreme head of the Roman Catholic Church, a Christian religion based in Rome.)

Machiavelli began his political career in 1498, when he was named chancellor (head administrator) and secretary of the Republic of Florence. He went on some twenty-three missions to foreign states. In 1503 he described his most memorable mission in a report titled "Description of the Manner Employed by Duke Valentino [Cesare Borgia] in Slaying Vitellozzo Vitelli, Oliverotto da Fermo, Signor Pagolo and the Duke of Gravina, Orsini." In great detail he described a series of political murders the notorious Spanish-born Italian nobleman Cesare Borgia (c. 1475–1507) ordered to eliminate his rivals. Machiavelli intended this work as a lesson in the art of politics for Florence's weak and indecisive leader, Pier Soderini. In 1510 Machiavelli was instrumental in organizing a militia (citizens' army) in Florence. In August 1512 the Florentines removed Soderini from office. Then the Medicis, who had previously ruled Florence, were able to return to power. Three months later Machiavelli was dismissed. Soon afterward he was arrested, imprisoned, and subjected to torture as an alleged conspirator against the Medicis. Though innocent, he remained a suspect for years. When he was unable to secure an appointment from the reinstated Medicis, he turned to writing political treatises, plays, and verse. In 1513 he wrote *The Prince*.

Niccolò Machiavelli wrote *The Prince,* **one of the most important works of the Renaissance period.**
©Bettmann/ Corbis. Reproduced by permission of Corbis Corporation.

Following are excerpts from chapters 14, 15, 17, and 18 of the *The Prince,* which are best known today as the heart of Machiavelli's political philosophy.

Things to Remember While Reading Excerpts from *The Prince:*

- "Prince" was the term used in the Renaissance to refer to a ruler.

- Machiavelli's chief innovation in *The Prince* was to view politics as a separate field. Since ancient times scholars and historians, including the humanists, had treated politics as a branch of moral philosophy.

- Fundamental to Machiavelli's theory were the concepts of *fortuna* (fortune) and *virtù* (virtue). Fortune, or chance, often determines a political leader's opportunity for decisive action. Yet Machiavelli, like others in the Renaissance, believed in *virtù,* the human capacity to shape destiny. This view contrasted sharply with the medieval concept of an all-powerful God and the ancient Greek belief that humans are powerless against fate. Machiavelli stressed the importance of *virtù,* which is unlike Christian virtue, or goodness, in that it is a combination of force and shrewdness—somewhat like a combination of the lion and the fox, with a touch of greatness.

- According to Machiavelli, the inborn badness of human beings requires that the prince instill fear rather than love in his subjects. When necessary the prince must also break his pledge with other princes, who will be no more honest than he. Machiavelli was attempting to describe rather than to invent the rules of political success. For him the needs of the state are greater than the individual interests of its citizens.

Excerpts from **The Prince**

CHAPTER XIV:
OF THE DUTY OF A PRINCE IN RESPECT OF MILITARY AFFAIRS

A Prince, therefore, should have no care or thought but for war, and for the regulations and training it requires, and should apply himself exclusively to this as his **peculiar province;** *for war is the sole art looked for in one who rules, and is of such* **efficacy** *that it not merely maintains those who are born Princes, but often enables men to rise to that* **eminence** *from a private station; while, on the other hand, we often see that when Princes devote themselves rather to pleasure than to arms, they lose their dominions. And as neglect of this art is the prime cause of such calamities, so to be a* **proficient** *in it is the surest way to acquire power....*

Between an armed and an unarmed man no **proportion** *holds, and it is contrary to reason to expect that the armed man should voluntarily submit to him who is unarmed, or that the unarmed man should stand secure among armed* **retainers.** *For with contempt on one side, and distrust on the other, it is impossible that men should work well together. Wherefore, as has already been said, a Prince who is ignorant of military affairs, besides other disadvantages, can neither be respected by his soldiers, nor can he trust them. A Prince, therefore, ought never to allow his attention to be diverted from warlike pursuits, and should occupy himself with them even more in peace than in war. This he can do in two ways, by practice or by study.*

As to the practice, he ought, besides keeping his soldiers well trained and disciplined, to be constantly engaged in the chase, that he may **inure** *his body to hardships and fatigue, and gain at the same time a knowledge of places, by observing how the mountains slope, the valleys open, and the plains spread; acquainting himself with the characters of rivers and marshes, and giving the greatest attention to this subject. Such knowledge is useful to him in two ways; for first, he learns thereby to know his own country, and to understand better how it may be defended; and next, from his familiar acquaintance with its localities, he readily comprehends the character of other districts when obliged to observe them for the first time.... The Prince who is* **wanting** *in this kind of knowledge, is wanting in the first qualification of a good captain, for by it he is*

Peculiar province: Exclusive responsibility.

Efficacy: Effectiveness.

Eminence: Position of prominence.

Proficient: Skilled.

Proportion: Equality.

Retainers: Servants or employees.

Inure: Accustom.

Wanting: Lacking.

*taught how to surprise an enemy, how to choose an **encampment**, how to lead his army on a march, how to array it for battle, and how to post it to the best advantage for a siege....*

As to the mental training of which we have spoken, a Prince should read histories, and in these should note the actions of great men, observe how they conducted themselves in their wars, and examine the causes of their victories and defeats, so as to avoid the latter and imitate them in the former. And above all, he should, as many great men of past ages have done, assume for his models those persons who before his time have been renowned and celebrated, whose deeds and achievements he should constantly keep in mind....

*A wise Prince, therefore, should pursue such methods as these, never resting idle in times of peace, but **strenuously** seeking to turn them to account, so that he may derive strength from them in the hour of danger, and find himself ready should Fortune turn against him, to resist her blows.*

CHAPTER XV:
OF THE QUALITIES IN RESPECT OF WHICH MEN,
AND MOST OF ALL PRINCES, ARE PRAISED OR BLAMED

*It now remains for us to consider what ought to be the conduct and bearing of a Prince in relation to his subjects and friends. And since I know that many have written on this subject, I fear it may be thought **presumptuous** in me to write of it also; the more so, because in my treatment of it I depart from the views that others have taken.*

*But since it is my object to write what shall be useful to whosoever understands it, it seems to me better to follow the real truth of things than an imaginary view of them. For many Republics and Princedoms have been imagined that were never seen or known to exist in reality. And the manner in which we live, and that in which we ought to live, are things so wide **asunder,** that he who quits the one to **betake** himself to the other is more likely to destroy than to save himself; since any one who would act up to a perfect standard of goodness in everything, must be ruined among so many who are not good. It is essential, therefore, for a Prince who desires to maintain his position, to have learned how to be other than good, and to use or not to use his goodness as necessity requires.*

Laying aside, therefore, all fanciful notions concerning a Prince, and considering those only that are true, I say that all men when they are spoken of, and Princes more than others from their being

Encampment: Military camp.

Strenuously: Vigorously.

Presumptuous: Overstepping reasonable bounds.

Asunder: Apart.

Betake: Cause oneself to go.

set so high, are characterized by some one of those qualities which attach either praise or blame. Thus one is accounted liberal, another miserly (which word I use, rather then avaricious, to denote the man who is too sparing of what is his own, avarice *being the disposition to take wrongfully what is another's*); one is generous, another greedy; one cruel, another tenderhearted; one **faithless,** another true to his word; one **effeminate** and cowardly, another high-spirited and courageous; one is courteous, another **haughty;** one impure, another chaste; one simple, another crafty; one firm, another **facile;** one grave, another **frivolous;** one devout, another unbelieving; and the like. Every one, I know, will admit that it would be most **laudable** for a Prince to be endowed with all of the above qualities that are reckoned good; but since it is impossible for him to possess or constantly practise them all, the conditions of human nature not allowing it, he must be discreet enough to know how to avoid the infamy of those **vices** that would deprive him of his government, and, if possible, be on his guard also against those which might not deprive him of it; though if he cannot wholly restrain himself, he may with less **scruple** indulge in the latter. He need never hesitate, however, to **incur** the reproach of those vices without which his authority can hardly be preserved; for if he well consider the whole matter, he will find that there may be a line of conduct having the appearance of virtue, to follow which would be his ruin, and that there may be another course having the appearance of vice, by following which his safety and well-being are secured.

CHAPTER XVII:
OF CRUELTY AND CLEMENCY,
AND WHETHER IT IS BETTER TO BE LOVED OR FEARED

Passing to the other qualities above referred to, I say that every Prince should desire to be accounted merciful and not cruel. Nevertheless, he should be on his guard against the abuse of this quality of mercy....

A Prince should therefore disregard the **reproach** of being thought cruel where it enables him to keep his subjects united and obedient. For he who **quells** disorder by a very few signal examples will in the end be more merciful than he who from too great **leniency** permits things to take their course and so to result in **rapine** and bloodshed; for these hurt the whole State, whereas the severities of the Prince injure individuals only....

And here comes in the question whether it is better to be loved rather than feared, or feared rather than loved. It might perhaps be

Faithless: Disloyal.

Effeminate: Like a woman.

Haughty: Proud.

Facile: Easy.

Frivolous: Silly.

Laudable: Praiseworthy.

Vices: Moral faults or failings.

Scruple: Ethical consideration that limits action.

Incur: Bring upon himself.

Reproach: Expression of disapproval.

Quells: Subdues.

Leniency: Tolerance.

Rapine: Seizure.

answered that we should wish to be both; but since love and fear can hardly exist together, if we must choose between them, it is far safer to be feared than loved. For of men it may generally be affirmed that they are thankless, **fickle,** false, studious to avoid danger, greedy of gain, devoted to you while you are able to confer benefits upon them, and ready, as I said before, while danger is distant, to shed their blood, and sacrifice their property, their lives, and their children for you; but in the hour of need they turn against you. The Prince, therefore, who without otherwise securing himself builds wholly on their professions is undone. For the friendships which we buy with a price, and do not gain by greatness and nobility of character, though they be fairly earned are not made good, but fail us when we have occasion to use them.

Moreover, men are less careful how they offend him who makes himself loved than him who makes himself feared. For love is held by the tie of obligation, which, because men are a sorry breed, is broken on every whisper of private interest; but fear is bound by the **apprehension** of punishment which never relaxes its grasp.

Nevertheless a Prince should inspire fear in such a fashion that if he do not win love he may escape hate. For a man may very well be feared and yet not hated, and this will be the case so long as he does not meddle with the property or with the women of his citizens and subjects. And if **constrained** to put any to death, he should do so only when there is **manifest** cause or reasonable justification. But, above all, he must abstain from the property of others. For men will sooner forget the death of their father than the loss of their **patrimony.** Moreover, **pretexts** for **confiscation** are never to seek, and he who has once begun to live by rapine always finds reasons for taking what is not his; whereas reasons for shedding blood are fewer, and sooner exhausted.

But when a Prince is with his army, and has many soldiers under his command, he must needs disregard the reproach of cruelty, for without such a reputation in its Captain, no army can be held together or kept under any kind of control. Among other things remarkable in **Hannibal** this has been noted, that having a very great army, made up of men of many different nations and brought to fight in a foreign country, no **dissension** ever arose among the soldiers themselves, nor any **mutiny** against their leader, either in his good or in his evil fortunes. This we can only **ascribe** to the **transcendent** cruelty, which, joined with numberless great qualities, rendered him at once **venerable** and terrible in the eyes of his soldiers;

Fickle: Changeable.

Apprehension: Fear or dread.

Constrained: Limited by force.

Manifest: Made clear.

Patrimony: Right to inheritance.

Pretexts: Pretenses.

Confiscation: Seizure.

Hannibal: (247–c. 183 B.C.E.) Carthaginian general who led his troops to victory over the Romans.

Dissension: Disagreement.

Mutiny: Rebellion.

Ascribe: Attribute to a supposed cause.

Transcendent: Supreme.

Venerable: Esteemed, respected.

for without this reputation for cruelty these other virtues would not have produced the like results....

Returning to the question of being loved or feared, I sum up by saying, that since his being loved depends upon his subjects, while his being feared depends upon himself, a wise Prince should build on what is his own, and not on what rests with others. Only, as I have said, he must do his utmost to escape hatred.

CHAPTER XVIII: HOW PRINCES SHOULD KEEP FAITH

Everyone understands how praiseworthy it is in a Prince to keep faith, and to live uprightly and not **craftily.** Nevertheless, we see from what has taken place in our own days that Princes who have set little store by their word, but have known how to overreach men by their cunning, have accomplished great things, and in the end got the better of those who trusted to honest dealing.

Be it known, then, that there are two ways of **contending,** one in accordance with the laws, the other by force; the first of which is proper to men, the second to beasts. But since the first method is often ineffectual, it becomes necessary to resort to the second. A Prince should, therefore, understand how to use well both the man and the beast....

But since a Prince should know how to use the beast's nature wisely, he ought of beasts to choose both the lion and the fox; for the lion cannot guard himself from the **toils,** nor the fox from the wolves. He must therefore be a fox to **discern** toils, and a lion to drive off wolves.

To rely wholly on the lion is unwise; and for this reason a **prudent** Prince neither can nor ought to keep his word when to keep it is hurtful to him and the causes which led him to pledge it are removed. If all men were good, this would not be good advice, but since they are dishonest and do not keep faith with you, you, in return, need to keep faith with them; and no Prince was ever at a loss for **plausible** reasons to cloak a **breach** of faith. Of this numberless recent instances could be given, and it might be shown how many solemn treaties and engagements have been rendered inoperative and idle through want of faith in Princes, and that he who has best known to play the fox has had the best success....

It is not essential, then, that a Prince should have all the good qualities which I have enumerated above, but it is most essential that he should seem to have them; I will even venture to affirm that

Craftily: Cleverly, cunningly.

Contending: Struggling against difficulties.

Toils: Nets to trap animals.

Discern: Detect.

Prudent: Wise.

Plausible: Believable.

Breach: Split.

if he has and invariably practises them all, they are hurtful, whereas the appearance of having them is useful. Thus, it is well to seem merciful, faithful, humane, religious, and upright, and also to be so; but the mind should remain so balanced that were it needful not to be so, you should be able and know how to change to the contrary.

And you are to understand that a Prince, and most of all a new Prince, cannot observe all those rules of conduct in respect whereof men are accounted good, being often forced, in order to preserve his Princedom, to act in opposition to good faith, **charity***, humanity, and religion. He must therefore keep his mind ready to shift as the winds and tides of Fortune turn, and, as I have already said, he ought not to quit good courses if he can help it, but should know how to follow evil courses if he must....*

Moreover, in the actions of all men, and most of all of Princes, where there is no **tribunal** *to which we can appeal, we look to results. Wherefore if a Prince succeeds in establishing and maintaining his authority, the means will always be judged honourable and be approved by every one. For the* **vulgar** *are always taken by appearances and by results, and the world is made up of the vulgar, the few only finding room when the many have no longer ground to stand on....*

What happened next...

Machiavelli also wrote *Discourses on the First Ten Books of Titus Livius,* which he had started before writing *The Prince.* His other works include *The Art of War and The Life of Castruccio Castracani* (1520); three plays, *The Mandrake, Clizia,* and *Andria; History of Florence* (1526); a short story, "Belfagor"; and several minor works in verse and prose. *Discourses* somewhat resembles *The Prince,* although Machiavelli sets forth his quarrel with the church in this work. He claimed the Italian states were weak and divided because the church was too feeble politically to dominate them but prevented any one state from uniting them. *The Mandrake* is considered the finest comedy of the Italian Renaissance. Scholars note that *History of Florence* was an advance over earlier histories because Machiavel-

Charity: Goodwill.

Tribunal: Court.

Vulgar: Common, lowly.

li traced underlying causes rather than the mere succession of events as he told the history of Florence after the death of Duke Lorenzo de' Medici in 1492.

Many of the positive values Machiavelli expressed in *The Prince* were adopted in the nineteenth century. Among them were the supremacy of the state over religion, the drafting of soldiers for citizen armies, and the preference for a republican government rather than a monarchy. Machiavelli was also instrumental in reviving the Roman ideals of honesty, hard work, and civic responsibility.

Did you know...

- Machiavelli is considered a sinister and ruthless politician, but many historians suggest this reputation is largely undeserved. They point out that Machiavelli lived by his own philosophy that a servant of government must be loyal and self-sacrificing. Furthermore, he never suggested that the political dealings of princes should be a model for day-to-day interactions among ordinary citizens.

- The main source of the misrepresentation of Machiavelli's ideas was the English translation, in 1577, of a work called *Contre-Machiavel* by the French Huguenot (Protestant) writer Gentillet. Gentillet distorted Machiavelli's teachings, which he blamed for the Saint Bartholomew's Day Massacre, the killing of Huguenots in Paris on a church holiday, in 1572. A poem by Gabriel Harvey the following year falsely attributed four principal crimes to Machiavelli: poison, murder, fraud, and violence. The negative image of Machiavelli was popularized by the crafty and greedy villain (evil person) Machiavel in *The Jew of Malta* (1588), a play by the English playwright Christopher Marlowe. Machiavellian villains followed in works by other playwrights.

For More Information

Books

Skinner, Quentin. *Machiavelli: A Very Short Introduction.* New York: Oxford University Press, 2000.

Thomson, Ninian Hill, and Daniel Fader, trans. *The Renaissance Man: Niccolò Machiavelli, "The Prince"; Baldassare Castiglione, "The Courtier."* New York: Grolier, 1969.

Vergani, Luisa. *"The Prince," Notes; Including Machiavelli's Life and Works.* Lincoln, Nebr., Cliff's Notes, 1967.

Viroli, Maurizio. *Niccolò's Smile: A Biography of Machiavelli.* Translated by Antony Shugaar. New York: Farrar, Straus and Giroux, 2000.

Web Sites

"Machiavelli, Nicolo." *Internet Philosophy Encyclopedia of Philosophy.* [Online] Available http://www.utm.edu/research/iep/m/machiave.htm, April 10, 2002.

"Machiavelli, Nicolò." *MSN Encarta.* [Online] Available http://encarta.msn.com/find/Concise.asp?ti=05DD9000, April 10, 2002.

Ibn Khaldûn

Excerpts from **The Muqaddimah** *(1377)*
Translated by Franz Rosenthal
Edited by N. J. Dawood
Published in 1989

The Renaissance is generally considered to be an era in European history only, yet a similar cultural and intellectual revolution took place in the Arab world. The greatest Arab figure of this period was the Muslim philosopher and historian 'Adb al-Rahman Ibn Khaldûn (known as Ibn Khaldûn; pronounced kal-DOON; 1332–1395). (A Muslim is a follower of Islam, a religion founded by the prophet Muhammad.) Ibn Khaldûn is best known today for *The Muqaddimah* (pronounced moo-kah-DEE-mah), which was the introduction to the first volume of *Kitāb al-'bar,* a history of the world.

Ibn Khaldûn completed *The Muqaddimah* in 1377, around the same time humanism (a movement devoted to the revival of ancient Greek and Roman culture) was gaining momentum in northern Italy. Like the European humanists, he used ancient Greek concepts to examine his own society and he placed humans at the center of the world. *The Muqaddimah* represented a significant leap forward in scholarship at the time. Unlike most philosophers who came before him, Ibn Khaldûn attempted to discover patterns in social and political organizations. (A philosopher was one who studied all learning except the technical and practical arts.) He used new scientific methods (systematic analysis based on direct observation) and terminology, which involved explaining and analyzing historical events instead of simply giving a chronological account. The Italian diplomat **Niccolò Machiavelli** (1469–1527; see entry) has been credited with introducing this technique in *The Prince* (1513), a description of the perfect ruler, and in his history of Florence, Italy (1526). Modern scholars note, however, that Ibn Khaldûn used the same approach more than one hundred fifty years earlier. In *The Muqaddimah* he identified psychological, economic, environmental, and social factors that contribute to the making of human civilization and history. Ibn Khaldûn is considered the pioneer of sociology (the science of society, social institutions, and social relationships), which was developed in the mid-nineteenth century. *The Muqaddimah* is now regarded as one of the great masterpieces of all time.

Ibn Khaldûn has long political career

Ibn Khaldûn came from an Arab family of scholars and politicians who originally lived in Yemen (a country on the southern edge of the Arabian Peninsula) before settling in Seville, a city in the Muslim-controlled region of Andalusia in southern Spain (see accompanying box). When Muslims were driven out of Andalusia in the early thirteenth century, Ibn Khaldûn's family moved to Tunis, the capital city of Tunisia in North Africa. Ibn Khaldûn was born in Tunis in 1332. While he was growing up his parents were active in the intellectual life of the city, associating with leading politicians and scholars from North Africa and Spain. Ibn Khaldûn was educated first by his father and then by prominent Muslim scholars. He memorized the Koran (holy book of Islam) and studied grammar (rules for use of a language), law, rhetoric (art of effective speaking and writing), philology (study of language in literary works), and poetry. In 1352, at the age of nineteen, Ibn Khaldûn entered the service of Sultan (king) Barquq, the Egyptian ruler of Tunis. This marked the beginning of Ibn Khaldûn's long political career. While serving with various rulers in Tunisia, Morocco, Algeria, and Spain, he acquired knowledge of politics and history that later formed the basis of his scholarly work.

Muslims in Spain

Ibn Khaldûn came from an Arab family of scholars and politicians who originally lived in Yemen before settling in Muslim-controlled Andalusia, the southern part of Spain. In C.E. 711 Muslims from Arabia and Berbers (non-Arab wandering tribes) from North Africa invaded Spain, where they were known as Moors. At the time of the Moorish invasion, Spain was occupied by Germanic tribes called Visigoths and Christianity was the dominant religion. After winning several major battles, the Moors conquered the Visigoth capital of Toledo in 712 and soon pushed the Germanic tribes into the northern frontiers of Spain. The Moors established a flourishing new culture based on their study of advanced civilizations of past times and their own era. Moorish farming techniques brought the dry land to life. Moorish architects renewed cities with intricately decorated mosques (Muslim houses of worship), lush gardens, and paved streets. They built the Great Mosque of the city of Córdoba in 786 and the Alhambra (a grand palace) in the city of Granada in the 1300s. The Moors introduced the secrets of making medicine and of producing steel, skills they had learned from the Far East (countries in Asia). Their philosophy made the cities of Córdoba, Granada, and Toledo important centers of learning.

Eventually feuds and disputes arose among the Muslim ruling families. In the eleventh century Christian states in the north of Spain took advantage of Muslim unrest and set out to recapture territories conquered by the Moors. The Moors surrendered Toledo to the Christians in 1085. In 1150 a new group of Berber conquerors, the Almohades, came to Spain. They controlled the Moorish regions until 1212, when they were defeated by Alfonso VIII of Castile at the battle of Navas de Tolosa. After that time, only Granada remained under Muslim control.

In 1354 Ibn Khaldûn left Tunis to join the ulama (religious council) in Fez, the capital of Morocco. While living in Fez he continued his studies and met the eminent scholars of the day. He also became involved in court politics, often taking sides as sultans fought for power in North Africa. He was imprisoned from February 1357 until November 1358 for participating in a plot to return an dethroned sultan to power in Algeria. Eventually Ibn Khaldûn rose to the position of chief justice of the ulama. After being denied the post of chamberlain (chief officer in the household of a king) in 1362, he decided to escape the political turmoil in North Africa. He moved to Granada, the only important Arab-controlled state

Moorish architects renewed cities with intricately decorated mosques, lush gardens, and paved streets. They built the Great Mosque of the city of Córdoba in 786. ©Vanni Archive/Corbis. Reproduced by permission of Corbis Corporation.

left in Spain. In 1364 the sultan of Granada, Ibn al-Ahmar, appointed Ibn Khaldûn head of a mission to meet with Peter the Cruel, the king of Castile, to seal a peace treaty between Castile and the Arabs. During his stay in Castile, Ibn Khaldûn visited Seville, the city of his ancestors. Peter invited Ibn Khaldûn to join the Castile court, offering to restore his family property, but Ibn Khaldûn declined the post. Ibn Khaldûn had become aware that his presence in Granada was arousing the jealousy of the Muslim scholar Ibn al-Khatib, who was Ibn al-Ahmar's prime minister (chief executive of a government). As a result, Ibn Khaldûn left Spain and returned to North Africa.

For the next decade Ibn Khaldûn had a precarious political career as warring rulers sought control of North Africa. Finally, in 1374 he and his family took refuge at Qalat Ibn Salama, a small village in the province of Oran in Algeria. Ibn Khaldûn devoted his time to writing *The Muqaddimah,* which he completed in 1377.

Things to Remember While Reading Excerpts from *The Muqaddimah:*

- Ibn Khaldûn followed in the tradition of the ancient Greek philosopher Plato (c. 428–348 or 347 B.C.E.). Like Plato, Khaldûn felt that the way an individual leads his or her life is directly related to the society as a whole. Both philosophers thought a virtuous person can exist only when the society is virtuous, but they also said that certain types of people were more fit to rule over society than others. Nevertheless, there was a significant difference between Plato and Ibn Khaldûn—Plato came up with his theory largely on his own, whereas Ibn Khaldûn's ideas were based on an established tradition. Plato described a perfect society in his famous work *The Republic.* He outlined laws and discussed how people should live, placing a "philosopher king" at the head of the society. Plato then wrote *The Laws,* which contained thousands of other laws to be used in his ideal society. Ibn Khaldûn did not have to do this. He based his concepts on the Koran, which provided an existing set of rules and laws. Moreover, the Koran was already the central text for the lives of millions of Muslims and could therefore be readily adopted. Ibn Khaldûn's method was a major innovation in the field of philosophy.

- Muslims regard the Koran as the perfect miracle because it was directly given to the prophet Muhammad (c. 570–632) by God. Unlike the Torah, the holy text of Judaism, and the New Testament, the holy text of Christianity, the Koran was not compiled over many years and subjected to changes by theologians. Instead, the Koran was immediately memorized by Muhammad's followers, who later wrote it down word for word as spoken by the prophet. Even today one can look at a Koran published in Russia and one printed in Africa, and the Arabic text will be exactly the same. Furthermore, a Koran written more than a thousand years ago contains the same text as one printed today.

- The following excerpts are from chapter 2 of *The Muqaddimah.* In sections 3 through 7 of that chapter Ibn Khaldûn explained why the Bedouins, Arab tribes that wander in the desert, were superior to people who have dwelled only in cities. He argued that the Bedouins lived closer to their own human nature and were therefore ideally suited to follow the teachings of Muhammad.

Excerpts from The Muqaddimah

3 Bedouins are **prior** to **sedentary** people. The desert is the basis and **reservoir** of civilization and cities

We have mentioned that the Bedouins restrict themselves to the bare necessities in their way of life and are unable to go beyond them, while sedentary people concern themselves with conveniences and luxuries in their conditions and customs. The bare necessities are no doubt prior to the conveniences and luxuries. Bare necessities, in a way, are basic, and luxuries secondary. Bedouins, thus, are the basis of, and prior to, cities and sedentary people. Man seeks first the bare necessities. Only after he has obtained the bare necessities does he get to comforts and luxuries. The toughness of desert life precedes the softness of sedentary life. Therefore, urbanization is found to be the goal to which the Bedouin aspires. Through his own efforts, he achieves what he proposes to achieve in this respect. When he has obtained enough to be ready for the conditions and customs of luxury, he enters upon a life of ease and submits himself to the **yoke** of the city. This is the case with all Bedouin tribes. Sedentary people, on the other hand, have no desire for desert conditions, unless they are motivated by some urgent necessity or they cannot keep up with their fellow city dwellers....

4 Bedouins are closer to being good than sedentary people

The reason for this is that the **soul** in its first natural state of creation is ready to accept whatever good or evil may arrive and leave an **imprint** upon it. Muhammad said: 'Every infant is born in the natural state. It is his parents who make him a Jew or a Christian or a **heathen.**' To the degree the soul is first affected by one of the two qualities, it moves away from the other and finds it difficult to acquire it. When customs proper to goodness have been first to enter the soul of a good person, and his (soul) has thus acquired the habit of (goodness, that person) moves away from evil and finds it difficult to do anything evil. The same applies to the evil person.

Prior: Came before.

Sedentary: Settled.

Reservoir: Place where something is stored.

Yoke: Bond.

Soul: Person's total self or spirit.

Imprint: Permanent memory.

Heathen: One who does not believe in God.

Renaissance and Reformation: Primary Sources

Sedentary people are much concerned with all kinds of pleasures. They are accustomed to luxury and success in worldly occupations and to **indulgence** in worldly desires. Therefore, their souls are coloured with all kinds of **blameworthy** and evil qualities. The more of them they possess, the more remote do the ways and means of goodness become to them. Eventually they lose all sense of **restraint**. Many of them are found to use improper language in their gatherings as well as in the presence of their superiors and womenfolk. They are not **deterred** by any sense of restraint, because the bad custom of behaving openly in an improper manner in both words and deeds has taken hold of them. Bedouins may be as concerned with worldly affairs as (sedentary people are). However, such concern would touch only the necessities of life and not luxuries or anything causing, or calling for, desires and pleasures. The customs they follow in their **mutual** dealings are, therefore, appropriate. As compared with those of sedentary people, their evil ways and blameworthy qualities are much less numerous. They are closer to the first natural state and more remote from the evil habits that have been impressed upon the souls (of sedentary people) through numerous and ugly, blameworthy customs. Thus, they can more easily be cured than sedentary people. This is obvious. It will later on become clear that sedentary life **constitutes** the last stage of civilization and the point where it begins to decay. It also constitutes the last stage of evil and of **remoteness** from goodness. Clearly, the Bedouins are closer to being good than sedentary people. . . .

5 Bedouins are more disposed to courage than sedentary people

The reason for this is that sedentary people have become used to laziness and ease. They are sunk in well-being and luxury. They have entrusted the **defence** of their property and their lives to the governor and ruler who rules them, and to the **militia** which has the task of guarding them. They find full assurance of safety in the walls that surround them, and the fortifications that protect them. No noise disturbs them, and no hunting occupies their time. They are carefree and trusting, and have ceased to carry weapons. **Successive** generations have grown up in this way of life. They have become like women and children, who depend upon the master of the house. Eventually, this has come to be a quality of character that replaces natural **disposition**.

The Bedouins, on the other hand, live apart from the community. They are alone in the country and remote from militias. They

Indulgence: Uncontrolled pleasure.

Blameworthy: Deserving blame.

Restraint: Control.

Deterred: Discouraged or prevented from action.

Mutual: Shared in common.

Constitutes: Make up, form.

Remoteness: Distance.

Defence: Defense.

Militia: Citizens organized for military service.

Successive: Following in order.

Disposition: Tendency.

have no walls or gates. Therefore, they provide their own defence and do not entrust it to, or rely upon others for it. They always carry weapons. They watch carefully all sides of the road. They take hurried naps only when they are together in company or when they are in the saddle. They pay attention to the most distant barking or noise. They go alone into the desert, guided by their **fortitude,** putting their trust in themselves. Fortitude has become a character quality of theirs, and courage their nature. They use it whenever they are called upon or roused by an alarm. When sedentary people mix with them in the desert or associate with them on a journey, they [sedentary people] depend on them. They cannot do anything for themselves without them. This is an observed fact. (Their dependence extends) even to knowledge of the country, the directions, watering places, and crossroads....

6 The reliance of sedentary people upon laws destroys their fortitude and power of resistance

Not everyone is master of his own affairs. Chiefs and leaders who are masters of the affairs of men are few in comparison to the rest. As a rule, man must by necessity be dominated by someone else. If the domination is kind and just and the people under it are not **oppressed** by its laws and restrictions, they are guided by the courage or **cowardice** that they possess in themselves. They are satisfied with the absence of any restraining power. Self-reliance eventually becomes a quality natural to them. They would not know anything else. If, however, the domination with its laws is one of **brute** force and **intimidation,** it breaks their fortitude and deprives them of their power of resistance as a result of the **inertness** that develops in the souls of the oppressed, as we shall explain.

When laws are (enforced) by means of punishment against someone who cannot defend himself generates in that person a feeling of **humiliation** that, no doubt, must break his fortitude.

When laws are (intended to serve the purposes of) education and instruction and are applied from childhood on, they have to some degree the same effect, because people then grow up in fear and **docility** and consequently do not rely on their own fortitude.

Thus, greater fortitude is found among the **savage** Arab Bedouins than among people who are subject to laws. Furthermore, those who rely on laws and are dominated by them from the very beginning of their education and instruction in the **crafts,** sciences, and religious matters, are thereby deprived of much of their own for-

Fortitude: Strength of mind that enables a person to encounter danger.

Oppressed: Crushed by abuse of power or authority.

Cowardice: A lack of courage.

Brute: Animal-like.

Intimidation: State of being frightened into submission.

Inertness: Inactivity.

Humiliation: Lowering of one's dignity.

Docility: Obedience.

Savage: Primitive, uncivilized.

Crafts: Occupations or trades requiring artistic skill.

Renaissance and Reformation: Primary Sources

titude. They can scarcely defend themselves at all against hostile acts. This is the case with students, whose occupation it is to study and to learn from teachers and religious leaders, and who constantly apply themselves to instruction and education in very dignified gatherings. This situation and the fact that it destroys the power of resistance and fortitude must be understood.

*It is no argument that men around Muhammad observed the religious laws, and yet did not experience any **diminution** of their fortitude, but possessed the greatest possible fortitude. When the Muslims got their religion from Muhammad, the restraining influence came from themselves, as a result of the encouragement and discouragement he gave them in the **Qur'ân.** It was not a result of technical instruction or scientific education. The laws were the laws and **precepts** of the religion that they received **orally** and which their firmly rooted belief in the truth of the articles of faith caused them to observe. Their fortitude remained **unabated,** and it was not **corroded** by education or authority....*

*(The influence of) religion, then, decreased among men, and they came to use restraining laws. The religious law became a branch of learning and a craft to be acquired through instruction and education. People turned to sedentary life and assumed the character trait of **submissiveness** to law. This led to a decrease in their fortitude....*

7 Only tribes held together by group feeling can live in the desert

It should be known that God put good and evil into the nature of man. Thus, He says in the Qur'ân: 'We led him along the two paths.' He further says: 'And inspired the soul with wickedness as well as fear of god.'

Evil is the quality that is closest to man when he fails to improve his customs and when religion is not used as the model to improve him. The great mass of mankind is in that condition, with the exception of those to whom God gives success. Evil qualities in man are injustice and mutual aggression. He who casts his eye upon the property of his brother will lay his hand upon it to take it, unless there is a restraining influence to hold him back. The poet thus says:

> *Injustice is a human trait. If you find*
> *A moral man, there is some reason why he is not unjust*

*Mutual aggression of people in towns and cities is **averted** by the authorities and the government, which hold back the masses*

Diminution: Decrease.

Qur'ân: Koran.

Precepts: General rules.

Orally: Spoken, instead of being written down.

Unabated: Being at full strength or force.

Corroded: Weakened.

Submissiveness: Permitting oneself to be subjected to something.

Averted: Turned away or aside.

under their control from attacks and aggression upon each other. They are thus prevented by the influence of force and governmental authority from mutual injustice, **save** such injustice as comes from the ruler himself.

Aggression against a city from outside may be averted by walls, in the event of unpreparedness, a surprise attack at night, or inability (of the inhabitants) to withstand the enemy during the day. Or it may be averted with the help of government **auxiliary** troops, if (the inhabitants are) prepared and ready to offer resistance.

The restraining influence among Bedouin tribes comes from their **shaykhs** and leaders. It results from the great respect and **veneration** they generally enjoy among the people. The **hamlets** of the Bedouins are defended against outside enemies by a tribal militia composed of noble youths of the tribe who are known for their courage. Their defence and protection are successful only if they are a closely knit group of common **descent.** This strengthens their **stamina** and makes them feared, since everybody's affection for his family and his group is more important (than anything else). Compassion and affection for one's blood relations and relatives exist in human nature as something God put into the hearts of men. It makes for mutual support and aid, and increases the fear felt by the enemy.

Those who have no one of their own **lineage** (to care for) rarely feel affection for their fellows. If danger is in the air on the day of battle, such a man slinks away and seeks to save himself, because he is afraid of being left without support. Such people, therefore, cannot live in the desert, because they would fall **prey** to any nation that might want to swallow them up.

If this is true with regard to the place where one lives, which is in constant need of defence and military protection, it is equally true with regard to every other human activity, such as **prophecy,** the establishment of royal authority, or **propaganda.** Nothing can be achieved in these matters without fighting for it, since man has the natural urge to offer resistance. And for fighting one cannot do without group feeling, as we mentioned at the beginning.

Save: Except.

Auxiliary: Reserve.

Shaykhs: Sheiks; chiefs.

Veneration: Respect or awe.

Hamlets: Towns.

Descent: Relation to an ancestor.

Stamina: Endurance.

Lineage: Family line.

Prey: Victim.

Prophecy: Utterance of divine inspiration; prediction of something to come.

Propaganda: Ideas, facts, or allegations deliberately spread to further a cause or to damage an opposing cause.

What happened next...

Continued unrest in North Africa made Ibn Khaldûn's political career uncertain. Finally, in 1382, he settled in Cairo, Egypt, where he spent the last twenty-four years of his life. Respected as a public figure and scholar, he was appointed chief judge of the Mâlikite community. Political opposition forced him out of office three times within five years. Nevertheless, he tried to fight corruption and favoritism, and he was serving as a judge at the end of his life. In 1383 Ibn Khaldûn completed *Kitāb al-'bar*. He also wrote poems, an autobiography (account of his own life), and a book on mathematics, and he lectured at Al-Azhar University as well as other universities. In 1400 Sultan Faraj of Egypt asked Ibn Khaldûn to accompany him on a military expedition to Damascus, a city in Syria and the center of the Arab world. It was about to be attacked by the Mongol conqueror Tamerlane (also called Timur; 1336–1405). After staying in Damascus for two weeks Faraj had to return to Cairo to put down a revolt. He left Ibn Khaldûn and Damascan leaders to deal with Tamerlane. Ibn Khaldûn was selected to conduct negotiations and he spent thirty-five days in the invader's camp. Tamerlane was so impressed with Ibn Khaldûn's arguments on behalf of Damascus that he freed the citizens before he raided the city. Ibn Khaldûn died in 1406 and was buried the Muslim cemetery outside Cairo.

Did you know...

- In 1382 Ibn Khaldûn went to Alexandria, Egypt, to make preparations for the *hajj*. The hajj is a pilgrimage (religious journey) to Mecca (the city in Saudi Arabia where Muhammad was born) that all Muslims are required to make at least once. When Ibn Khaldûn was unable to join the caravan bound for Mecca, he turned toward Cairo instead. He received a warm welcome from the academic community and spent the rest of his life in the city. Ibn Khaldûn finally made his pilgrimage to Mecca in 1387.

- In 1384 Ibn Khaldûn's family died when the ship carrying them from Tunis sank near the harbor of Alexandria.

For More Information

Books

Ibn Khaldûn, 'Adb al-Rahman. *The Muqaddimah: An Introduction to History.* Translated by Franz Rosenthal. Edited by N. J. Dawood. Princeton, N.J.: Princeton University Press, 1989.

Web Sites

"Ibn Khaldûn." *Columbia Encyclopedia.* [Online] Available http://www.bartleby.com/cgi-bin/texis/webinator/sitesearch/?query=khaldun&db=db&cmd=context&id=38d47ecd1af#hit1, April 10, 2002.

Marvin, Christ. "Ibn Khaldûn: Iranian Muslim Philosopher." [Online] Available http://www.trincoll.edu/depts/phil/philo/phils/muslim/khaldun.html, April 10, 2002.

Renaissance Arts and Science

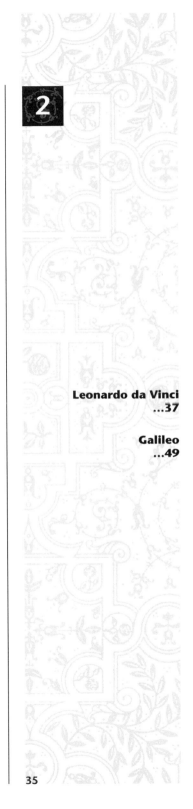

The Renaissance was an era of unparalleled innovation and creativity in painting, sculpture, and architecture, especially in Italy, which was the home of Renaissance art. Inspired by humanist concepts, many artists perfected their talents in several areas, personifying the ideal of the "Renaissance man." One of the most famous multitalented figures was the Italian artist Leonardo da Vinci. He not only produced masterpieces in painting and sculpture but also worked as an engineer and inventor. In fact, for Leonardo art and science were closely related. Throughout his career he kept notebooks in which he wrote down his ideas on a wide range of subjects, including theories of painting, ideas for remarkably modern inventions, and plans for houses and towns.

At the height of the Renaissance a scientific revolution was initiated by astronomers who introduced new ways of understanding their world in relation to the heavens. Rejecting the traditional theory of an Earth-centered universe, these scientists set out to test the theory that the Earth revolves around the Sun. One of the most important developments was the invention of the telescope, which enabled astronomers to gain a closer view of the orbits of planets and the positions of stars. The seventeenth-century Italian scientist Galileo Galilei was the first to use the telescope to observe the Moon, planets, and groups of stars. He reported his findings in *The Starry Messenger,* in which he described how he made his telescope and gave details of his radically new observations of the surface of the Moon.

Leonardo da Vinci

Excerpts from Notebooks *(c.1490–1515)*

Reprinted in *Selections from the Notebooks of Leonardo da Vinci*

Edited by Irma A. Richter
Published in 1977

The Italian Renaissance was a time of experimentation in painting, sculpture, and architecture. During the Middle Ages (c. 400–1400; also known as the medieval period) the artist was an anonymous vehicle for glorifying God. In the Renaissance, however, human beings became the central focus of artistic expression. This development was the result of the humanist movement, a revival of the culture of ancient Greece and Rome (called the classical period) initiated by scholars in Florence, Italy, in the mid-1300s. Humanists believed that a body of learning called *studia humanitatis* (humanistic studies), which was based on the literary masterpieces from the classical period, could bring about a cultural rebirth, or renaissance. Humanists were committed to the revival of ancient works, which emphasized human achievement, as a way to end the "barbarism" (lack of refinement or culture) of the Middle Ages.

The Renaissance art movement began in the early fifteenth century when humanist ideas were put into practice by painters, sculptors, and architects in Florence. Using a human-centered approach, they started a revolution that quickly spread to other Italian city-states such as Urbino, Ferrara, Padua, Mantua, Venice, and Milan. Renaissance art is divided into three periods: early Renaissance (1420–95), High Renaissance (1495–1520), and mannerism (also called the late Renaissance; 1520s–1600). These periods overlapped, depending on the artists and the places where they worked. Renaissance art theories began reaching other European countries in the 1500s, at the peak of the High Renaissance. Around this time Rome became the artistic capital of Europe.

As the Renaissance gained momentum the artist achieved a new status as a creative genius. Prior to this time artists occupied the position of artisans, or craftsmen, and were considered socially inferior to the upper classes. Now wealthy patrons, or financial supporters, clamored to commission the greatest artists, who gained coveted posts in the courts of monarchs and the nobility. As part of the revival of classical culture, Renaissance artists studied ancient ruins in Rome and adapted ancient painting techniques. They also introduced their own innovations, such as the use of linear perspective. Invented by the Florentine architect Filippo Brunelleschi (1377–1446), linear perspective is a system derived from mathematics in which all elements of a composition are measured and arranged from a single point of view, or perspective. The Florentine artist Masaccio (Tommaso di Giovanni di Simone Guidi; 1401–1428), known as the father of Renaissance painting, was the first to use linear perspective extensively. Portraits of prominent people and their families also became increasingly popular, reflecting a dramatic shift from the idea that heavenly figures or saints were the only worthy subjects of art. In addition, landscape painting was emerging as a new genre, or form of art. This was another important change, because in medieval art nature was simply the environment of human beings and therefore had little significance.

Leonardo introduces new techniques

One of the greatest figures of the High Renaissance was Leonardo da Vinci (1452–1519), a painter, sculptor, engineer, and scientist. He began his career as a painter in Florence, then worked in Milan and Rome before moving permanently to France during his final years. He also served as a military engineer while working as an artist. Leonardo produced many paintings, but only a few have survived. Nevertheless, he introduced techniques that influenced other painters. An example is *Adoration of the Magi* (1481), which is based on the story of the three Magi (kings; wise men) who traveled to Bethlehem from the East (ancient Persia; present-day Iran) to pay homage to the newborn Jesus Christ (later the founder of Christianity). Leonardo used a new approach by depicting human drama through an effect of continuing movement. A crowd of spectators, with odd and varied faces, flutters around and peers at Mary (mother of Jesus), who is holding the baby Jesus. In the background the three Magi are mounted on horses that prance among intricate architectural ruins. Traditionally, in paintings of this story Mary and Jesus had appeared at one side of the picture and the Magi approached from the other side. Leonardo departed from tradition by placing Mary and Jesus in the center of the composition. He also used linear perspective to depict the ruins in the background.

Painter, sculptor, engineer, and scientist Leonardo da Vinci was one of the greatest figures of the High Renaissance period.
Photograph courtesy of The Library of Congress.

While working in Milan, Leonardo painted *Virgin of the Rocks* (1480s), another highly original work. He used the tradition of showing Mary and Jesus in a cave. This gave him the opportunity to experiment with dimmed light, which is coming from two sources, one behind the cave and the other in front of it. (Leonardo once wrote that an artist should practice drawing at dusk and in courtyards with walls painted black.) The technique highlights the four figures—Mary and Jesus and another woman and infant—in a soft, shadowy atmosphere. *Last Supper* (1495–97), a later painting that Leonardo did in Milan, depicts Jesus' final meal with his twelve disciples, or followers. For this fresco (wall painting) Leonardo decided not to use the traditional water-based paint, which makes areas of color appear distinct and does not allow for shading. Instead, he experimented with oil-based paint, which is more easily blended, but his efforts were unsuccessful. The paint did not adhere well to the wall, and within fifty years the scene became a confused series of spots. *Last Supper* was an important work, however, because it represented another new approach. Earlier Renaissance artists had applied the rules of linear perspective to show that objects appear smaller as they are farther away from the eye of the viewer. Leonardo combined this principle with two others: the perspective of clarity (distant objects gradually lose their separateness and hence are not drawn with outlines) and perspective of color (distant objects gradually take on gray tones). He wrote about both of these techniques in his notebooks.

In 1503 he was invited to paint a large-scale fresco that celebrated the Battle of Anghiara, in which Florence defeated Milan in 1440. The fresco was to be painted on the walls of the newly built Council Chamber of the Republic in the Palazzo della Signoria in Florence. Leonardo experimented with an oil-based paint on a primed (prepared with a sealing substance) wall surface. This process proved to be ineffective because the paint did not dry. The central section of the composition, which was destroyed during a restoration project in 1565, is now known through numerous copies made during the sixteenth and seventeenth centuries. Shortly after Leonardo began the *Battle of Anghiara* his younger rival, Michelangelo Buonarroti (known as Michelangelo; 1475–1564), was commissioned to paint *Battle of Cascina,* another celebrated Florentine victory, for the same room in the Palazzo della Signoria. In 1503, while working on the Anghiara project Leonardo started painting the *Mona Lisa.* It is a portrait of Lisa di Anton Giocondo, the young wife of the prominent Florentine citizen Francesco del Giocondo. The *Mona Lisa* became one of the most famous portraits in European art because of Lisa's mysterious smile, which is in the process of either appearing or disappearing.

Records ideas in notebooks

In the 1490s Leonardo began keeping notebooks in which he recorded his ideas on a wide range of topics. He also illustrated the notebooks with drawings that demonstrated his ideas. He was working on the notebooks when he died in 1519. Following are five excerpts from Leonardo's notebooks, which reflect his ideas on art and the wide range of his interests.

Things to Remember While Reading Excerpts from *Selections from the Notebooks of Leonardo da Vinci:*

- Leonardo was particularly interested in science, which for him was closely related to art. For instance, he studied anatomy in order to understand the human form so he could paint realistic figures. The first excerpt is a series of notes he made on the ideas of the ancient Roman architect and engineer Marcellus Vitruvius Pollio (called Vitruvius; first century B.C.E.), who studied the proportions of the human body. Leonardo illustrated the proportions in his famous drawing *Vitruvian Man* (1492).

- Leonardo's famous fresco *Battle of Anghiara* was destroyed, but copies were made during the sixteenth and seventeenth centuries. As indicated in a copy made by the Flemish painter Peter Paul Rubens in 1615, Leonardo depicted the extreme physical exertion of men and horses engaged in furious battle. The group of central figures displays faces distorted by rage or pain. Even the heads of the horses, with flaring nostrils and gnashing teeth, were treated in this expressive manner. The second notebook excerpt, in which Leonardo gave detailed instructions on painting a battle scene, shows how he may have achieved the effects in *Battle of Anghiara.*

- In the third excerpt Leonardo reflected the Renaissance view of the artist as a creative genius. Notice that he believed painting could not be taught, and that the artist has a special talent for giving an exact representation of nature. Leonardo ranked painting as a science, even suggesting a comparison between the artist and God. This was a revolutionary idea, because in the Middle Ages artists had been considered ordinary craftsmen who were inferior to scientists and other thinkers. Also the artist was regarded as a mere vehicle for reflecting the glory of God, but, like the Renaissance humanists, Leonardo elevated the painter to the position of supreme creator.

- Leonardo had a lifelong interest in architecture. Although no buildings designed by him are known to exist, he was involved in designing and planning various architectural projects. The fourth notebook excerpt is his plan for a house. Notice that each part of the house has a specific function, which fits harmoniously into the entire space.

- Leonardo designed many mechanical devices. His best-known invention was a flying machine, which he designed by observing bird flight and the motions of air. The fifth excerpt is the notes he wrote about his flying machine.

Excerpts from *Selections from the Notebooks of Leonardo da Vinci*

Vitruvian man

Vitruvius, the architect, says in his work on architecture that the measurements of the human body are distributed by nature as follows: 4 fingers make 1 palm; 4 palms make 1 foot; 6 palms make 1 cubit; 4 cubits make a man's height; and 4 cubits make one pace; and 24 palms make a man; and these measures he used in buildings.

If you open your legs so much as to decrease your height by 1/14 and spread and raise your arms so that your middle fingers are on a level with the top of your head, you must know that the navel will be the centre of a circle of which the outspread limbs touch the circumference; and the space between the legs will form an equilateral triangle.

The span of a man's outspread arms is equal to his height.

The way to represent a battle

Represent first the smoke of the artillery, mingled in the air with the dust tossed up by the movement of horses and combatants.... The smoke will assume a bluish tinge, and the dust will keep to its colour. This mixture of air, smoke, and dust will look much lighter from the side whence the light comes than from the opposite side. The more the combatants are in this turmoil the less will they be seen, and the less will be the contrast between their lights and shadows. You should give a ruddy glow to the faces and figures and the air around them, and to the gunners and those near them.... And if you make horses galloping away from the throng, make the little clouds of dust distant from each other as is the space between

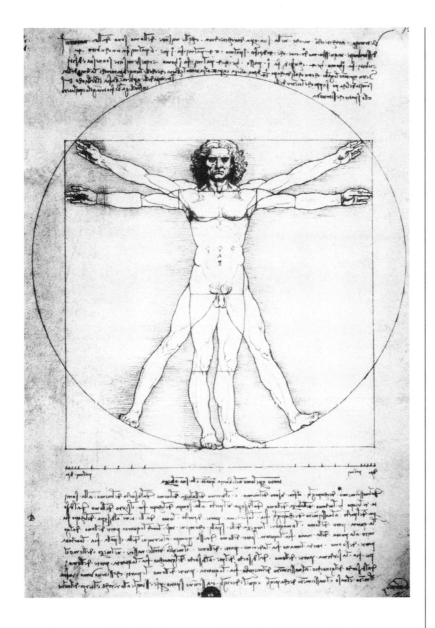

the strides made by the horse, and that cloud which is farthest away from the horse should be least visible, for it should be high and spread out and thin, and the nearer should be more conspicuous, smaller and denser. Let the air be full of arrows in every direction, some shooting upwards, some falling, some flying level. The balls from the guns must have a train of smoke following their course. The figures in the foreground you must make with dust on their hair and eyebrows and on such other flat places likely to retain it. You will make the conquerors rushing onwards with their hair and other light things streaming in the wind, with brows bent down; and they should be thrusting forward the opposite limbs; that is if a man advances the right foot, the left arm should also come forward. And if you make anyone fallen you must make the mark where he has slipped on the dust turned into blood-stained mire; and round about in the half-liquid earth show the print of the trampling of men and horses who have passed that way. Make a horse dragging the dead body of his master, and leaving behind him in the dust and mud the track where the body was dragged along.... Show someone using one hand as a shield for his terrified eyes with the palm turned towards the enemy; while the other rests on the ground to support his half-raised body. Represent others shouting with their mouths wide open, and running away. Put all sorts of arms between the feet of the combatants, such as broken shields, lances, broken swords, and other objects. Make the dead partly or entirely covered with dust, which is mingled with the oozing blood and changed into crimson **mire,** and let the blood be seen by its colour flowing in a **sinuous** stream from the corpse to the dust. Others in the death agony grinding their teeth, rolling their eyes, with their fists clenched against their bodies, and the legs distorted.... You might see a riderless horse charging with mane streaming in the wind among the enemy and doing him great mischief with his hoofs. You may see some **maimed** warrior fallen on the ground, covering himself with his shield, and the enemy bending down over him and trying to give him the death-stroke. There might also be seen a number of men fallen in a heap on top of a dead horse....

You will see the **squadrons** of the **reserves** standing full of hope and watchful with eyebrows raised, shading them with their hands peering into the thick and confusing mist in readiness for the command of the captain; and so too the captain, with **staff** raised, hurrying to the reserves, pointing out to them the quarter where they are needed. And show a river wherein horses are galloping stirring up the water all around with turbulent waves, and foam, and broken water, leaping into the air and over the legs and bodies of the horses. And see to it that you paint no level spot of ground that is not trampled with blood.

"The painter is lord"

The painter is lord of all types of people and of all things. If the painter wishes to see beauties that charm him it lies in his power to create them, and if he wishes to see monstrosities that are frightful,

Mire: Slush.

Sinuous: Snakelike, winding.

Maimed: Seriously injured or crippled.

Squadrons: Military units.

Reserves: Military forces to be used later in battle.

Staff: Rod carried as a symbol of authority.

buffoonish or ridiculous, or pitiable he can be lord and god thereof; if he wants to produce inhabited regions or deserts or dark and shady retreats from the heat, or warm places in cold weather, he can do so. If he wants valleys, if he wants from high mountain tops to unfold a great plain extending down to the sea's horizon, he is lord to do so; and likewise if from low plains he wishes to see high mountains.... In fact whatever exists in the universe, in essence, in appearance, in the imagination, the painter has first in his mind and then in his hand; and these are of such excellence that they can present a proportioned and harmonious view of the whole, that can be seen simultaneously, at one glance, just as things in nature.

He who despises painting loves neither philosophy nor nature. If you despise painting, which is the sole imitator of all the visible works of nature, you certainly will be despising a subtle invention which brings philosophy and subtle speculation to bear on the nature of all forms—sea and land, plants and animals, grasses and flowers, which are enveloped in shade and light. Truly painting is a science, the true-born child of nature, for painting is born of nature, but to be more correct we should call it the grandchild of nature; since all visible things were brought forth by nature and these her children have given birth to painting. Therefore we may justly speak of it as the grandchild of nature and as related to God.

Painting cannot be taught to those not endowed by nature, like mathematics where the pupil takes in as much as the master gives. It cannot be copied like letters where the copy has the same value as the original. It cannot be moulded as in sculpture where the cast is equal in merit to the original; it cannot be reproduced indefinitely as is done in the printing of books.

Plan of house

A building ought always to be detached all round in order that its true shape can be seen.

Large room for the master, room, kitchen, **larder,** guardroom, large room for the family, and hall.

The large room for the master and that for the family should have the kitchen between them, and in both the food may be served through wide and low windows or by tables that turn on swivels. The large room of the family is on the other side of the kitchen so that the master of the house may not hear the clatter.

The wife should have her own apartment and hall apart from that of the family, so that she may set her serving maids to eat at

Buffoonish: Foolish.

Larder: Place where food is stored.

another table in the same hall. She should have two other apartments as well as her own, one for the serving maids, the other for the nurses, and ample space for their utensils. And the apartment will be in communication with the various conveniences; and the garden and stable in contact.

*He who is stationed in the **buttery** ought to have behind him the entrance to the kitchen, in order to be able to do his work expeditiously; and the window of the kitchen should be facing the buttery so that he may extract the wood. And let the kitchen be convenient for cleaning **pewter** so that it may not be seen being carried through the house. I wish to have one door to close the whole house.*

Flying machine

The genius of man may make various inventions, encompassing with various instruments one and the same end; but it will never discover a more beautiful, more economical, or a more direct one than nature's, since her inventions nothing is wanting and nothing is superfluous.

*A bird is an instrument working according to the mathematical law, which instrument it is in the capacity of man to reproduce with all its movements but not with as much strength, though it is deficient only in power of maintaining **equilibrium.** We may therefore say that such an instrument constructed by man is lacking nothing except the life of the bird, and this life must needs be imitated by the life of man. The life which resides in the bird's members will without doubt better obey their needs than will that of man which is separated from them and especially in the almost **imperceptible** movements which preserve equilibrium. But since we see that the bird is equipped for many sensitive varieties of movement, we are able from this experience to deduce that the most obvious of these movements will be capable of being comprehended by man's understanding, and that he will to a great extent be able to provide against the destruction of that instrument of which he has made himself life and guide.*

Buttery: Storeroom or pantry.

Pewter: Utensils made of pewter, a metal containing tin and lead.

Equilibrium: State of balance.

Imperceptible: Extremely subtle.

What happened next...

Leonardo had considerable influence on artists of his own day and later times. Some of his views on art, which had

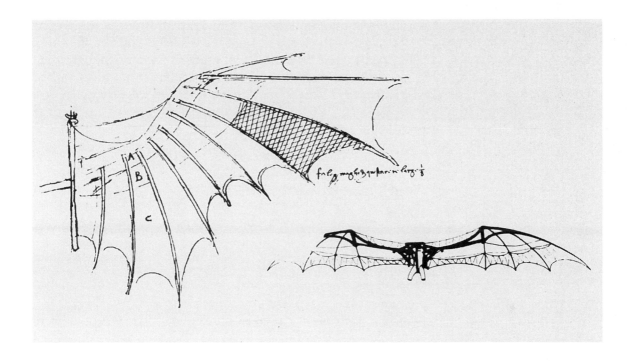

been circulating since the sixteenth century, were published in 1651 in *Trattato della pittura* (Treatise on painting). This is a collection of his writings taken from numerous manuscripts. The small number of Leonardo's surviving paintings show his achievements as an artist. He made contributions to every artistic form, from portraits to religious narratives. He gave new insights into figure grouping, space, individual characterization, and light and shade. Many of his works inspired copies. In Florence his compositions were carefully studied by the great painter Raphael. Leonardo's *Battle of Anghiara* and Michelangelo's design for *Battle of Cascina* were the "school for the world," in the words of Italian sculptor Benvenuto Cellini (1500–1571). Even in the nineteenth century, long after *Battle of Anghiara* had disappeared, aspects of its design continued to intrigue artists throughout Europe.

A drawing of Leonardo's best-known invention, a flying machine, which he designed by observing bird flight.

Did you know...

- Leonardo designed a submarine. He wrote in his notebook, however, that he would "not publish or divulge [the design] on account of the evil nature of men who would practise assassinations at the bottom of the seas by breaking the ships in their lowest parts and sinking them together with the crews who are in them; although I will furnish particulars of others which are not dangerous, for above the surface of the water emerges the mouth of a tube by which they draw breath, supported upon wine skins or pieces of cork."

For More Information

Books

Gelb, Michael. *How to Think Like Leonardo Da Vinci: Seven Steps to Genius Every Day.* New York: Delacorte Press, 1998.

Lafferty, Peter. *Leonardo da Vinci.* New York: Bookwright, 1990.

Nuland, Sherwin B. *Leonardo da Vinci.* New York: Viking, 2000.

Richter, Irma A., ed. *Selections from the Notebooks of Leonardo da Vinci.* New York: Oxford University Press, 1977.

Video Recordings

Masterpieces of Italian Art. Volume: Da Vinci, Michelangelo, Raphael and Titian. New York: VPI-AC Video Inc., 1990.

Web Sites

"Leonardo da Vinci." *Artcyclopedia.* [Online] Available http://artcyclopedia. com/artists/leonardo_da_vinci.html, April 10, 2002.

"Leonardo da Vinci," *MSN Encarta.* [Online] Available http://encarta. msn.com/find/Concise.asp?z=1&pg=2&ti=761561520, April 10, 2002.

"Leonardo da Vinci." *National Museum of Science and Technology.* [Online] Available http://www.museoscienza.org/english/leonardo/leonardo. html, April 10, 2002.

Pioch, Nicolas. "Leonardo da Vinci." *WebMuseum.* [Online] Available http://mexplaza.udg.mx/wm/paint/auth/vinci/, April 10, 2002.

Galileo Galilei

Excerpt from **The Starry Messenger (1610)**
Reprinted in *The Achievement of Galileo*
Edited by James Brophy and Henry Paolucci
Published in 1962

A scientific revolution occurred during the Renaissance through the influence of humanists who took a renewed interest in the work of ancient philosophers. Humanism was a movement initiated in Florence, Italy, in the mid-1300s by scholars who set out to revive the culture of ancient Greece and Rome (called the classical period). They hoped to start a cultural rebirth, or renaissance, that would end what they believed was the "barbarism" of the Middle Ages, the thousand-year period that began with the fall of the Roman Empire in the fourth and fifth centuries. Scientists were particularly interested in giving Greek texts updated translations and interpretations. They developed new theories that eventually replaced the Greek concepts that had dominated science for almost two thousand years. By the sixteenth century science had become a separate field from philosophy and technology, which had been the major areas of thought in ancient times. (Philosophy is devoted to a search for a general understanding of values and reality through speculative thinking. Technology is the application of practical knowledge, such as engineering.) An even more important development was that science now had a practical function. For instance, scientists were asking *how* things happened in nature, whereas the ancients were mainly concerned with *why* things happened. This shift in thinking had a profound impact on all aspects of life, and by the end of the 1600s science had replaced Christianity (a religion founded by Jesus of Nazareth, called the Christ) as the center of European civilization.

The most significant advances took place in the field of astronomy, the study of the number, size, and motions of heavenly bodies. At the beginning of the Renaissance astronomy was still linked with cosmology and astrology as it had been since ancient times. Cosmology is the study of the nature of the universe as an ordered structure, and it is closely allied with philosophy and theology (the study of religious faith, practice, and experience). Astrology is the "science" of the influences of heavenly bodies on earthly matters, including the lives and fortunes of humans. Some of the most famous Renaissance views of the universe, such as infinity (unlimited time and space), were developed not by astronomers but by philosophers and theologians (those who study religion). These ideas were then incorporated into astronomy. In fact, the scientific revolution began in astronomy, with the work of Polish astronomer Nicolaus Copernicus (1473–1543).

In 1543 Copernicus published *De revolutionibus orbium coelestium* (On the Revolution of the Heavenly Spheres), in which he gave proof that the Sun is the center of the universe. This idea was extremely controversial. At the time all astronomers accepted the theory of the ancient Egyptian scholar Ptolemy (Claudius Ptolemaeus; c. C.E. 100–c. 170), who stated that the Sun revolved around the Earth. Moreover, this view was enforced by the Roman Catholic Church, which found evidence for it in the Bible (the Christian holy book). Copernicus died only a few hours after *De revolutionibus orbium coelestium* was printed, however, and his work went virtually unnoticed for decades. Then in 1604 the Italian astronomer Galileo Galilei (called Galileo; 1564–1642) publicly declared that he supported Copernicus's theory of a Sun-centered universe.

A professor of physical sciences (study of the Earth and the universe) at the University of Padua in the Republic of Venice, Galileo had been attracting attention since he joined the faculty in 1592. At that time he gave three public lectures before overflow audiences in Venice. He argued that a new star, which had appeared earlier that year, was major evidence in support of Copernicus's views. More important was a letter in which he stated his theory of natural motion. By natural motion Galileo meant that a body will fall freely in space, and he proposed the law of free fall to account for this phenomenon. This concept contradicted the accepted view that the universe was a perfectly ordered and fixed system in which no body can freely move on its own.

In 1609 Galileo learned about the success of some Dutch spectacle, or eyeglass, makers in combining lenses (pieces of glass that reflect images) into what later came to be called the telescope. He feverishly set to work, and on August 25 he presented to the Venetian Senate a telescope as his own invention. The success was tremendous. He obtained a lifelong contract at the University of Padua, but he also stirred up resentment when it was learned that he was not the original inventor. Within a few months, however, Galileo had made sensational discoveries, which he published on March 12, 1610, under the title *Sidereus nuncius* (The Starry Messenger). The booklet took the world of science by storm.

Italian astronomer Galileo began to gain public attention after asserting that he supported Nicolaus Copernicus's view of a Sun-centered universe.
©Bettmann/Corbis. Reproduced by permission of Corbis Corporation.

Things to Remember While Reading an Excerpt from *The Starry Messenger:*

- The telescope was a revolutionary scientific advancement. Prior to the development of telescopic lenses, astronomers had to rely on observations with the naked eye and on mathematical calculations when they studied stars and planets. Although some of their data were accurate, they could usually make only speculations because there was no way to have a close view of distant objects.

- In *The Starry Messenger* Galileo gave astonishing evidence about mountains on the Earth's Moon and about moons circling Jupiter. He also identified a large number of stars, especially in the belt of the Milky Way, a galaxy (very large group of stars), of which the Earth's solar system is a part.

- In the following excerpt from *The Starry Messenger* Galileo described how he made his telescope. He then detailed his observations of the surface of the Moon, which he found to be rough and uneven. This was an important discovery because astronomers at the time accepted the theory of the ancient Greek philosopher Aristotle (384–322 B.C.) that the surface of the Moon is perfectly smooth.

Excerpt from The Starry Messenger

*About ten months ago a report reached my ears that a certain **Fleming** had constructed a spyglass by means of which visible objects, though very distant from the eye of the observer, were distinctly seen as if nearby. Of this truly remarkable effect several experiences were related, to which some persons gave **credence** while others denied them. A few days later the report was confirmed to me in a letter from a noble Frenchman at Paris, Jacques Badovere, which caused me to apply myself wholeheartedly to inquire into the means by which I might arrive at the invention of a similar instrument. This I did shortly afterwards, my basis being the theory of **refraction**. First I prepared a tube of lead, at the ends of which I fitted two glass lenses, both **plane** on one side while on the other side one was **spherically convex** and the other **concave.** Then placing my eye near the concave lens I perceived objects satisfactorily large and near, for they appeared three times closer and nine times larger than when seen with the naked eye alone. Next I constructed another one, more accurate, which represented objects as enlarged more then sixty times. Finally, sparing neither labor nor expense, I succeeded in constructing for myself so excellent an instrument that objects seen by means of it appeared nearly one thousand times larger and over thirty times closer than when we regarded with our natural vision.*

*It would be **superfluous** to enumerate the number and importance of the advantages of such an instrument at sea as well as on*

Fleming: A Dutch lens maker.

Credence: Willingness to believe.

Refraction: Change in the direction of light.

Plane: Flat.

Spherically convex: Rounded, protruding shape.

Concave: Sunken.

Superfluous: Unnecessary.

land. But forsaking **terrestrial** observations, I turned to celestial ones, and first I saw the moon from as near at hand as if it were scarcely two terrestrial **radii** away. After that I observed often with wondering delight both the planets and the fixed stars, and since I saw these latter to be very crowded, I began to seek (and eventually found) a method by which I might measure their distances apart.

Now let us review the observations made during the past two months, once more inviting the attention of all who are eager for true philosophy to the first steps of such important contemplations. Let us speak first of that surface of the moon which faces us. For greater clarity I distinguished two parts of this surface, a lighter and a darker; the lighter part seems to surround and to **pervade** the whole **hemisphere,** while the darker part discolors the moon's surface like a kind a cloud, and makes it appear covered with spots. Now those spots which are fairly dark and rather large are plain to everyone and have been seen throughout the ages; these I shall call the "large" or "ancient" spots, distinguishing them from others that are smaller in size but so numerous as to occur all over the **lunar surface,** and especially the lighter part. The latter spots had never been seen by anyone before me. From observations of these spots repeated many times I have been led to the opinion and conviction that the surface of the moon is not smooth, uniform, and precisely spherical as a great number of philosophers believe it (and the other heavenly bodies) to be, but is uneven, rough, and full of cavities and **prominences,** being not unlike the face of the earth, relieved by chains of mountains and deep valleys. The things I have seen by which I was enabled to draw this conclusion are as follows.

On the fourth or fifth day after new moon, when the moon is seen with brilliant horns, the boundary which divides the dark part from the light does not extend uniformly in an oval line as would happen on a perfectly spherical solid, but traces out an uneven, rough, and very wavy line.... Indeed, many luminous **excrescences** extend beyond the boundary into the darker portion, while on the other hand some dark patches invade the illuminated part. Moreover a great quantity of small blackish spots, entirely separated from the dark region, are scattered almost all over the area illuminated by the sun with the exception only of that part which is occupied by the large and ancient spots. Let us note, however, that the said small spots always agree in having their blackened parts directed toward the sun, while on the side opposite the sun they are crowned with bright contours, like shining summits. There is a similar sight on

Terrestrial: Having to do with the surface of the Earth.

Radii: Plural of radius; line segments extending from the center of a circle.

Pervade: Spread over.

Hemisphere: Half of a sphere- or ball-shaped object.

Lunar surface: Surface of the Moon.

Prominences: Raised areas.

Excrescences: Projections.

earth about sunrise, when we behold the valleys not yet flooded with light though the mountains surrounding them are already ablaze with glowing splendor on the side opposite the sun. And just as the shadows in the hollows on earth diminish in size as the sun rises higher, so these spots on the moon lose their blackness as the illuminated region grows larger and larger.

*Again, not only are the boundaries of shadow and light in the moon seen to be uneven and wavy, but still more astonishingly many bright points appear within the darkened portion of the moon, completely divided and separated from the illuminated part and at a considerable distance from it. After a time these gradually increase in size and brightness, and an hour or two later they become joined with the rest of the lighted part which has now increased in size. Meanwhile more and more peaks shoot up as if sprouting now here, now there, lighting up within the shadowed portion; these become larger, and finally they too are united with that same **luminous** surface which extends ever further. And on the earth, before the rising of the sun, are not the highest peaks of the mountains illuminated by the sun's rays while the plains remain in shadow? Does not the light go on spreading while the larger central parts of those mountains are becoming illuminated? And when the sun has finally risen, does not the illumination of plains and hills finally become one? But on the moon the variety of elevations and **depressions** appears to surpass in every way the roughness of the terrestrial surface....*

What happened next...

The view of the heavens changed drastically, and so did Galileo's life. In 1610 he accepted the position of mathematician in Florence, Italy, at the court of Duke Cosimo II de' Medici (1590–1621). Galileo's move to Florence turned out to be highly unwise. In the beginning everything went well. He made a triumphal visit to Rome in 1611, and the next year his *Discourse on Bodies in Water* was published. In this work he disclosed his discovery of the phases of the planet Venus, which proved the truth of the Copernican theory that celestial bodies travel around the Sun. Galileo's aim was to make a detailed description of the universe according to the theories of Copernicus and to develop a new form of physics (a science that deals with energy and matter and their interaction). A major obstacle was the traditional belief, stated in the Bible,

Luminous: Glowing.

Depressions: Sunken areas.

"A Grand Revolution"

At the conclusion of *The Starry Messenger* Galileo summarized evidence that supported the Copernican theory of a universe with the Sun, not the Earth, at its center. In an amused tone he noted that some people were quite happy to accept the idea that planets revolve around the Sun. Yet they seemed to be offended by any notion that the Earth might move around the Sun along with the planets.

Galileo wrote:

Here we have a fine and elegant argument for quieting the doubts of those who, while accepting with tranquil mind

the revolutions of the planets about the sun in the Copernican system, are mightily disturbed to have the moon alone revolve about the earth and accompany it in an annual rotation about the sun. Some have believed that this structure of the universe should be rejected as impossible. But now we have not just one planet rotating about another while both run through a great orbit around the sun; our own eyes show us four stars which wander around Jupiter as does the moon around the earth, while all together trace out a grand revolution about the sun in the space of twelve years.

Brophy, James, and Henry Paolucci, eds. The Achievement of Galileo, p. 28.

that the Earth is the center of the universe. To deal with the difficulties raised by the Scripture (text of the Bible), Galileo addressed religious issues. He was assisted by church leaders, such as Monsignor Piero Dini and Father Benedetto Castelli, his best scientific pupil. In letters to Dini and Castelli, Galileo produced essays that now rank among the best writings of biblical analysis of those times. His longest letter was addressed to Grand Duchess Christina of Tuscany. In all of the letters he discarded the idea of an Earth-centered universe in favor of the theory that the Earth revolves around the Sun. As the letters were more widely circulated, a confrontation with church authorities became inevitable. In 1616 Cardinal Robert Bellarmine issued an order that forbade Galileo from teaching, printing, or defending the Copernican doctrine of the motion of the Earth.

Galileo agreed not to promote Copernicus's views. Nevertheless, he was determined to have the order overturned. The next year Galileo had six audiences, or formal meetings, with Pope Urban VIII (1568–1644; reigned 1623–44). Urban promised a pension for Galileo's son, Vincenzio, but he did not grant Galileo permission to resume his work on a new description of the universe. Before departing for Florence, Galileo was informed that the pope had remarked that he did not believe the Roman Catholic Church would ever declare the Copernican theory to be heretical, but he was also certain the theory could never be proven. This news gave Galileo encouragement to go ahead with the great undertaking of his life, the *Dialogue concerning the Two Chief World Systems.*

Galileo's *Dialogue* was published in 1632. The book features four main topics discussed by three speakers in dialogue, or conversation, form on four consecutive days. The speakers are Simplicius, Salvati, and Sagredo. Simplicius represents Aristotle, Salviati is a spokesman for Galileo, and Sagredo plays the role of an arbiter (one who makes the final judgment on an issue), who leans heavily toward Galileo. The first day is devoted to the criticism of the alleged perfection of the universe, as claimed by Aristotle. Here Galileo made use of his discovery of the "imperfections" of the Moon, namely, its rugged surface as revealed by the telescope. The second day is a discussion of the rotation of the Earth on its axis (an imaginary line extending through the center of the Earth from north to south) as an explanation of various aspects of the universe. During the third day the orbital motion of the Earth around the Sun is debated. A main issue is the undisturbed nature of the surface of the Earth in spite of its double motion— that is, its revolving on an axis while at the same time orbiting around the Sun. The discussion on the fourth day shows that the tides (the rhythmical rising and falling of oceans and other bodies of water) are proof of the Earth's twofold motion. In this section Galileo seems to contradict the contention of the third day discussion, that the surface of the Earth remains undisturbed by its double motion. The tides, which cause the regular movement of oceans, show that the Earth's surface is in fact affected by the twofold motion.

Put on trial by church

Church officials were outraged by the *Dialogue,* which proved that Galileo supported Copernicus's ideas. Galileo was summoned to Rome to appear before the Inquisition, a church court set up to punish heretics (those who violate the laws of God and the church). The proceedings dragged on

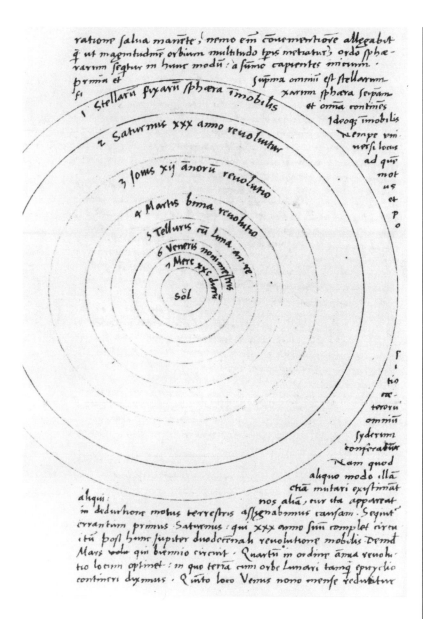

The handwritten Latin text within the image reads (as transcribed from Copernicus's manuscript):

ratione salua manente, nemo em conuenientiore allegabit
q ut magnitudinis orbium multitudo tpis metiatur, ordo sphæ-
rarum sequitur in hunc modum: a summo capientes initium.
prima et
fi ↑ Stellaru fixaru sphæra imobilis
2 Saturnus XXX anno reuoluitur
3 Ioms xij anoru reuolutio
4 Martis bima reuolutio
5 Telluris cu Luna an. re
6 Veneris noni mensis
7 Merc xxc diem
Sol
summa omniu est stellarum
xarium sphæra seipam
et omnia continens
Ideoq imobilis
nempe vni
uersi locus
ad que
mot
us
et
po
                    r
                    i
                    tio
                    re
                    terorum
                    omniu
                    syderum
                    conseratur
                    Nam quod
aliquo modo illa
ctia mutari existimat
aliqui: nos alia, cur ita appareat
in deductione motus terrestris assignabimus causam. Sequutur
errantium primus Saturnus: qui xxx anno suu complet circu
itu post hunc Iupiter duodecennali reuolutione mobilis Demd
Mars qui biennio circuit. Quartu in ordine annua reuolutio locum optinet: in quo terra cum orbe Lunari tanq epicyclio
contineri diximus. Quinto loco Venus nono mense reducitur

from the fall of 1632 to the summer of 1633. During that time Galileo was allowed to stay at the home of the Florentine ambassador in Rome. He was never subjected to physical force, but he had to inflict torture upon himself by publicly rejecting the doctrine that the Earth moved around the Sun. In 1633 *Dialogue* was placed on the Index of Prohibited Books by the Holy Office. The Holy Office was a branch of the church established as part of the Inquisition to review the content of all publications. The Index of Prohibited Books was a list of works the church considered to be heretical.

After the trial Galileo was placed under house arrest (not permitted to leave the premises) in Siena, a province in western Italy. The following December he was given permission to live in his own villa (country house) at Arcetri, a village near Florence. He was not supposed to have any visitors, but this order was not obeyed. The church was also unable to prevent the printing of Galileo's works outside Italy. Over the next five years translations of his writings were published in France and Holland. But the most important event in this connection took place in 1638, when Galileo's *Two New Sciences* was printed in Leiden, Holland. Like the *Dialogue,* this work is in the form of discussions over a period of four days. Topics include the mechanical resistance of materials, the atomic composition of matter, the nature of vacuum, the vibrations of pendulums, uniform and accelerated motion, and the projectile motion of a cannonball. Galileo spent his last years partially blind. He died in 1642.

Did you know...

- Although Galileo proposed a radically new concept of the universe, he remained a Christian to the end of his life. He believed that the world was made by a rational creator (God) who gave order to everything according to weight, measure, and number. Galileo stated this faith in the closing pages of the first day of the *Dialogue.* He described the human mind as the most excellent product of the creator, because it could recognize mathematical truths.

- In 1820 the condemnation of Copernicanism was revoked, or withdrawn, by the Holy Office. This action was taken on the basis of discoveries made by two little-known Italian astronomers. The first, Giovanni Battista Guglielmini, offered proof of the Earth's rotation by conducting experiments with bodies falling from a high tower. In Bologna, between 1789 and 1792, he made measurements and observed that the bodies moved slightly to the east, thus proving that the Earth moves in a twofold motion. The second astronomer, Giuseppe Calendrelli, measured the parallax (an apparent change in

Galileo performing his legendary experiment dropping a cannonball and a wooden ball from the top of the Leaning Tower of Pisa. This experiment was designed to prove that objects of different weights fall at the same speed. *Reproduced by permission of Hulton Archive.*

an object's position caused by a change in the position of the observer) of star Alpha in the constellation Lyra, also confirming such motion. He presented his findings to Pope Pius VII in a work published in 1806. During a debate over whether to approve an astronomy text in 1820, Benedetto Olivieri, head of the Holy Office, determined that the experiments of Guglielmini and Calendrelli demonstrated the Earth's twofold movement. As a result of Guglielmini's and Calendrelli's findings, Galileo's *Dialogue* was finally removed from the Index of Prohibited Books in 1835.

• On November 10, 1979, Pope John Paul II (1920– ; elected 1978) acknowledged that Galileo had suffered a great deal from the church. The pope called for a frank reexamination of the famous trial. On July 3, 1981, he appointed a special commission to study and publish all available documents relating to the trial. The pope presented the results of the commission's work to the Pontifical (pope's) Academy of Sciences on October 31, 1992. The report made clear that astronomy was in a state of transition when Galileo was silenced in 1616 and when he was forced to withdraw his theory in 1633. Furthermore, scripture scholars were confused about cosmology. The report stated that Galileo had not demonstrated the Earth's motion, and theologians had been mistaken in their assessment of his teachings. But in the 1990s, the pope continued, science was so complex it was almost impossible to certify scientific discoveries as being absolutely true. The best one can hope for, he said, is that discoveries be "seriously and solidly grounded." He went on to state that the function of the Pontifical Academy was to advise the church if the degree of probability of a discovery is such "that it would be imprudent [unwise] or unreasonable to reject it." In other words, a scientific discovery should not be rejected if there is any possibility that it can be proven.

For More Information

Books
Brophy, James, and Henry Paolucci, eds. *The Achievement of Galileo.* New York: Twayne, 1962.

Fisher, Leonard Everett. *Galileo.* New York: Macmillan, 1992.

Goldsmith, Mike. *Galileo Galilei.* Austin, Tex.: Raintree Steck-Vaughn, 2001.

Milton, Jacqueline. *Galileo: Scientist and Stargazer.* New York: Oxford University Press, 2000.

Sound Recordings
Sis, Peter. *Starry Messenger.* Prince Frederick, Md.: Recorded Books, 1997.

Video Recordings
Galileo: On the Shoulders of Giants. Devine Entertainment, 1997.

Web Sites
Art of Renaissance Science: Galileo and Perspective. [Online] Available http://www.crs4.it/Ars/arshtml/arstoc.html, April 10, 2002.

"Galileo." *MSN Encarta.* [Online] Available http://encarta.msn.com/find/ Concise.asp?z=1&pg=2&ti=017E5000, April 10, 2002.

Galileo Galilei. [Online] Available http://galileo.imss.firenze.it/museo/b/ egalilg.html, April 10, 2002.

Drama and Literature

During the Renaissance playwrights expanded popular the-atrical forms—such as religious plays, comedies, satires, romances, revenge dramas, history plays, and court masques —to create new genres that depicted human conflicts and predicaments. Aided by the printing press, authors wrote a steady stream of plays that portrayed important social issues of the day and attracted audiences in record numbers. The center of this phenomenon was Elizabethan England, where many great playwrights produced masterpieces that continue to be performed today. One of the most popular English play-wrights was William Shakespeare, and one of his best-known works is the comedy *The Merchant of Venice.* In this play Shakespeare appealed to sixteenth-century prejudices against Jews with his portrayal of the character Shylock, a Jewish money lender.

Renaissance writers produced many literary works that are now considered classics. One of the earliest was *Hep-taméron* by the French author Margaret of Navarre, duchess of Angoulême. With this collection of tales Margaret popular-ized the novella, a form that was introduced in the Middle

Ages (c. 400–1450), and produced a complex narrative featuring women. The most famous work of fiction from the Renaissance period—and one of the masterpieces of world literature—is *Don Quixote* by the Spanish writer Miguel de Cervantes. This comic epic about the errant, or traveling, knight Don Quixote of la Mancha was largely responsible for creating what is known as the modern novel. The Renaissance was also a time of experimentation in literature. The French author Michel Eyquem de Montaigne created a new literary genre, the essay, in which he used self-portrayal as a mirror of humanity in general. Among Montaigne's best-known essays is "Of Cannibals," in which he contemplated the recently discovered society of cannibals in Brazil in the New World. A unique contribution to English literature of the late Renaissance was *The Description of a New World Called the Blazing World* by Margaret Cavendish, first duchess of Newcastle. The story of a young lady who becomes the warrior queen of a fantasy world, this work is regarded as one of the first science fiction novels.

William Shakespeare

Excerpt from **The Merchant of Venice** *(1596)*

Edited by Brents Stirling
Published in 1987

The playwright William Shakespeare (1564–1616) is considered the greatest of English writers and one of the most talented creators in history. Today he is the most quoted author in the English language. Shakespeare had established his career in London by 1592, when theater was flourishing in England. He was popular with audiences from a wide range of social classes, who flocked to see his plays. At the time of his retirement in 1613 he had made important innovations in all the major dramatic genres, or forms, of the Renaissance period—comedy (depiction of humorous characters and situations), romance (love story), chronicle (history play), and tragedy (drama portraying the downfall of a good man).

Shakespeare's earliest plays were comedies, which entertained audiences while depicting social issues of the day. One of his best-known comedies is *The Merchant of Venice,* which he wrote as a "comicall history," that is, a play with a happy ending. The central character is Shylock, a greedy, scheming Jewish banker who cares only about money. Shylock is meant to be a comic figure, and in the "happy" ending is his conversion to Christianity. (Conversion is the act of rejecting

William Shakespeare

William Shakespeare was born in Stratford-upon-Avon, a market town in Warwickshire, England, in 1564. Historians know little about his early life. His father, John, was a successful leather merchant and prominent citizen in Stratford. His mother, Mary Arden, was the daughter of a prosperous landlord in a nearby village. William most likely learned to read and write either at home or in a "petty" (elementary) school. Around the age of seven he probably enrolled at King's New School in Stratford, where he would have read ancient Latin works. He never attended a university. Instead, in November 1582 at age eighteen he married Anne Hathaway (c. 1556–1623), a Stratford woman who was eight years older than he. They had a daughter, Susanna, six months later. William and Anne may not have been happy together, but they did have two other children, twins named Hamnet and Judith, in 1585. Shakespeare had to rely on his own resources to support his family, though his occupation is not known. It is certain, however, that by 1592 he was in London, evidently without his family. He gained a reputation as a playwright and actor, and when he retired in 1613 he had made major innovations in all the dramatic forms of the Renaissance period. He died in 1616, at age fifty-two. Shakespeare's value to his own age is suggested by the fact that, in 1623, two fellow actors gathered his plays together and published them in a form known as the Folio edition. Without their efforts many of the plays would not have survived, since Shakespeare was not interested in publication.

one's religion and accepting another.) From the perspective of the twenty-first century, the portrayal of Shylock may not seem amusing and his forced conversion may be considered morally offensive. Yet Shakespeare was reflecting commonly held sixteenth-century attitudes toward Jews, who were intensely mistrusted by Christians. In fact, as a result of anti-Semitic, or anti-Jewish, prejudices Jews had been subjected to expulsions (forced exits) from European countries for centuries. When *The Merchant of Venice* was first performed in 1596 (published 1600), thousands of Jews had been driven out of many areas and they were allowed to live only in certain places.

Jews confined to northern and central Italy

Jews arrived in western Europe around A.D. 300, and over the next several centuries Christians became increasingly hostile toward them. This attitude was heavily influenced by the image of the Jews as murderers of Christians and the killers of Jesus Christ, the founder of Christianity. It was called the blood libel. According to the blood libel, Jews killed Christian boys to use their blood for "magical" rituals such as circumcision (removal of the foreskin of the penis) and the baking of unleavened (without yeast) bread called Passover matzos, which were eaten during the celebration of the ancient Hebrews' liberation from slavery in Egypt. Circumcision and the baking of unleavened bread were ancient practices of the Jewish religion, but Christians associated these rituals with sorcery (use of magic to activate evil spirits). Although there was no basis for believing in the blood libel, Christians throughout Europe intensely feared Jews. Between 1290 and about 1655, Jews were not legally allowed to live in England. After riots against Jews in Spain in 1391, Jews were massacred and all survivors were forced to convert to Christianity. These New Christians (*conversos;* the converted) were commonly called Marranos, the Spanish word for pigs.

By the 1400s Jews were living in Spain, Portugal, Italy, the Low Countries (Belgium, Luxembourg, and the Netherlands), and Germany, yet they were under extreme pressure either to convert to Christianity or to leave Europe. In 1492, during the Spanish Inquisition (a Catholic Church court established to seek out and punish non-Christians), all unconverted Jews were expelled from Spain. In 1497 the Jews of Portugal were converted, then forced out of the country by the Portuguese Inquisition in the 1530s. The Jews of Sicily, which was under Spanish rule, were forced to flee, and those of the Kingdom of Naples were ousted by 1541. Jews living in Germany were either driven out or subjected to constant attack. Jews of the Low Countries lived under cover as Christians until the seventeenth century. Any Jews remaining in Europe lived exclusively in northern and central Italy.

Jews valued as merchants, traders, and bankers

The threat of expulsion was not the only factor that affected the lives of Jews. They were not permitted to practice most professions, such as law and medicine. There was a widely held belief that they wanted to take over the world and were seeking to dominate important professions as a way to stamp out Christianity. Since the Middle Ages (c. 400–1450), Jews had been limited to working as merchants (those who sell goods) and traders (those involved in buying and selling goods), yet many became quite wealthy. During the Renaissance successful Jewish merchants and traders served on the courts of Italian rulers. Through their connections with Jewish traders in the Ottoman Empire, European Jews were ideally suited to supply armies with grain, timber, horses, and cattle. They also supplied Italian rulers with diamonds, precious stones, and other luxury items. Jews were valued for their organizational skills. Rulers turned to individual Jews who were able to offer reliable, speedy, and extensive supplies of foodstuffs, cloth, and weapons for the army, the central instrument of a ruler's power. Court Jews were often employed as tax administrators and court minters (those who made coins), and they engaged in secret and delicate political negotiations. Having formed strong personal bonds with rulers, court Jews were entrusted with arranging transfers of credit for them as well as providing financial assistance.

During the Renaissance, Jews gained prominence as bankers in the major cities of northern and central Italy. They formed communities based on a *condotta,* a limited contract that allowed small groups of Jews to settle in a city and establish banks for providing loans to the poor. Jews settled in Venice, Italy, in 1516, but only within an area long known as the Ghetto Nuovo (new ghetto; the origin of the term "ghetto"). In the 1530s the pope (head of the Roman Catholic Church) issued a condotta that permitted Portuguese Jews to settle in Venice and Ferrara in order to promote commerce and international trade. These Jewish communities were essentially collections of individuals who were given authority by outside rulers to administer Jewish internal affairs—and to

collect taxes. They were allowed to base their communities on Jewish law, but their autonomy, or right to self-rule, was limited. For instance, the pope was constantly interfering in the work of Jewish tribunals, or courts, even to the point of instructing these tribunals how to interpret Jewish law. In 1631 Venetian authorities discovered that Jewish laws held the threat of excommunication (being expelled from the community) for any Jews who turned to non-Jewish courts. The Venetians then accused the Jews of trying to operate their own republic within the Republic of Venice.

The Merchant of Venice

The Merchant of Venice is set in Venice, and the main plot (story line) revolves around the attempts of two young Italians, Antonio and Bassanio, to convince Shylock to give them a loan. Shylock drives a hard bargain, however, and demands harsh terms. The play opens with Antonio, a merchant in Venice, talking with his friend Bassanio. Bassanio was once rather wealthy, but he is no longer rich because he made poor financial decisions. He owes quite a bit of money, particularly to Antonio. Bassanio thinks the best way to regain his wealth is to marry a wealthy woman. He has recently received word that a woman named Portia, who lives in Belmont, has been left with a great deal of money after her father's death. She is continually visited by a great many suitors, but Bassanio is convinced he can win her heart and her money. However, he needs money to make the trip. Antonio wants to help, but all of his funds are tied up in merchandise that is being shipped throughout Europe. Antonio tells Bassanio the solution to his problem is to borrow money on credit from a lender in Venice.

Winning Portia's hand in marriage will not be a simple task. She is not permitted to choose a husband herself. Her father's will states that her future husband will be the man who makes the correct choice among three chests: one filled with gold, one with silver, and one with lead. Upon picking the chest, the man must give the reason for his choice. The man who picks the right chest for the right reason wins Portia and her inheritance. Portia is dismayed that she can neither dismiss any of her suitors nor accept one of them based on her own preferences.

"An equal pound"

As Portia laments her fate, Bassanio and Antonio attempt to secure a loan from Shylock, the Jew. In Act I, scene iii, Antonio and Bassanio try to convince Shylock to lend them the money. Shylock does not want to, saying that Antonio and Bassanio call him names behind his back and spit upon him in public. He asks why he should then turn around and give them something they need. Finally, Shylock agrees to lend the money on one condition: if Antonio and Bassanio have not made full payment in three months, Shylock can take one pound of flesh from any part of Antonio's body that he, Shylock, wishes. Shylock's "pound of flesh speech" is an important part of the play, as well as one of the best-known passages in English drama. He says:

This Kindness will I show:

Go with me to a notary; seal me there

Your single bond, and—in a merry sport—

If you repay me not on such a day,

In such a place, such sums as are

Expressed in the condition, let the forfeit

Be nominated for an equal pound

Of your fair flesh, to be cut off and taken

In what part of your body pleaseth me.

Antonio agrees to these conditions because ships carrying his merchandise will soon land at their designated ports and he will be immensely wealthy. Bassanio then sets out for Belmont to try to win Portia. In the next scene, Portia is visited by a number of suitors. One picks the golden chest, for gold is the greatest of all precious metals, much like Portia is the greatest of all beauties. This choice is incorrect, so Bassanio has a good chance of winning her. He continues his journey while another suitor picks the chest of silver. This choice too is incorrect. As Portia's suitors continue to unravel the riddle of her father's will, Shylock is facing a tragedy of his own. His daughter Jessica has run away with a Christian man, Lorenzo, and has taken with her a fair amount of Shylock's money. Shylock believes she is on the ship chartered by Antonio and Bassanio, although people in town tell Shylock she is not. Dismissing their advice, Shylock is determined to find Jessica.

Act III, scene i, which is reprinted below, opens after one of Antonio's ships has been shipwrecked.

Things to Remember While Reading an Excerpt from *The Merchant of Venice:*

- Salerio and Solanio, friends of Antonio and Bassanio, inform Shylock of the recent events and attack him for his business practices. They claim that Shylock has none of the virtues possessed by his daughter Jessica. Shylock retorts with the now famous speech beginning with the line "Hath a Jew not eyes," in which he argues that Jews are just as human as Christians. Shylock's friend Tubal then enters and tells Shylock he has been unable to find Jessica, yet he has heard that she is spending all of the money she stole. Tubal also informs Shylock that another of Antonio's ships has been wrecked. This brings Shylock much joy. He is certain that Antonio is now destitute and cannot repay his bond. At the end of the scene, Shylock eagerly departs, bent on taking a pound of flesh from Antonio's body.

- Shakespeare's plays are always complicated and intricate. Twenty-first-century readers find the language difficult to understand, and some of the cultural references are no longer relevant to present-day society. It might be helpful to think of Shakespeare's plays as being similar to some television comedies we watch today. An example is *Saturday Night Live*. Like Shakespeare, the writers of this popular program create exaggerated situations and characters. They use satire (criticism expressed through humor) as a way of making fun of politicians, celebrities, and recent events in the news. Yet the humor of *Saturday Night Live* often has a serious side, giving the viewer insight into human weaknesses and absurd behavior.

- Christian forgiveness and mercy are represented by Antonio, Bassanio, and Portia. Shylock, on the other hand, fits the sixteenth-century stereotype of Jews as cold-hearted people who had no sense of mercy or forgiveness. This is evident in the play when the Christian characters constantly ask Shylock to show mercy or forgiveness, especially in regard to the debt owed to him by Antonio. Many scholars have interpreted this as Christian characters trying to force Shylock to convert to Christianity and forsake his own religion.

- Shylock's "Hath a Jew not eyes" speech, in the middle of Act III, scene i, has frequently been interpreted as Shakespeare's plea for tolerance toward Jews. Scholars believe this interpretation is inaccurate, saying that Shylock was not meant to be a sympathetic character. Throughout the play he is ridiculed for being Jewish, and the stereotypes associated with Jews are personified in his character. By having Shylock insist on having a "pound of flesh" from Antonio, Shakespeare made a comment on usury, or charging extremely high interest rates (percentage of the amount of money borrowed). At that time the practice of usury was part of the stereotype of Jewish money lenders. Whether the interest rates charged by Jews were any higher than those charged by Christians is still being debated by scholars.

- Notice that Shylock does not seem concerned that Jessica has gone missing. He is more worried about the loss of his money. The only thing that makes him feel better is knowing that Antonio will be unable to repay the debt. In Jewish culture, family is the center of life and Shylock would not be expected to act this way. Shakespeare was again using the Jewish stereotype by having Shylock show a lack of concern about his daughter yet great love for his money.

Excerpt from The Merchant of Venice

[Act III, scene i]

[Enter] Solanio and Salerio

SOLANIO *Now what news on the* **Rialto**?

SALERIO *Why, yet it lives there* **unchecked** *that Antonio hath a ship of rich* **lading wracked** *on the narrow seas—the Goodwins I think they call the place, a very dangerous flat, and fatal, where the* **carcasses** *of many a tall ship lie buried as they say, if my* **gossip Report** *be an honest woman of her word.*

SOLANIO *I would she were as lying a gossip in that as ever* **knapped** *ginger or made her neighbors believe she wept for the death of a third husband. But it is true, without any slips of* **prolixity** *or crossing the plain highway of talk, that the good Antonio, the honest Antonio—O that I had a title good enough to keep his name company!—*

SALERIO *Come, the full stop!*

SOLANIO *Ha, what sayest thou? Why the end is, he hath lost a ship.*

SALERIO *I would it might prove the end of his losses.*

SOLANIO *Let me say amen betimes* **lest** *the devil* **cross** *my prayer, for there he comes in the likeness of a Jew.*

Enter Shylock.

How now, Shylock? What news among the merchants?

Rialto: Street in Venice.

Unchecked: Unrestrained.

Lading: Cargo.

Wracked: Ruined.

Carcasses: Bodies.

Gossip Report: Dame Rumor.

Knapped: Nibbled.

Prolixity: Wordiness.

Lest: In case.

Cross: Cancel.

Withal: With.

Fledge: Ready to fly.

Dam: Mother.

Carrion: Dead and rotting flesh.

Jet: Velvet-black coal often used for jewelry.

Ivory: Creamy white substance from the tusk of an animal such as an elephant.

Rhenish: From the Rhine River region in Germany.

Bankrout: Bankrupt; lacking funds to pay bills and expenses.

Prodigal: Reckless, extravagant.

Smug: Self-satisfied.

Mart: Market.

Bond: Agreement to repay borrowed money.

Wont: Accustomed.

Usurer: One who charges an extremely high fee for loaning money.

Cursy: As a Christian courtesy.

Hind'red: Hindered.

Thwarted: Prevented.

Dimensions: Physical traits.

Sufferance: Patient endurance.

Villainy: Evil or vile behavior.

SHYLOCK *You knew, none so well, none so well as you, of my daughter's flight.*

SALERIO *That's certain. I for my part knew the tailor that made the wings she flew* **withal.**

SOLANIO *And Shylock for his own part knew the bird was* **fledge,** *and then it is the complexion of them all to leave the* **dam.**

SHYLOCK *She is damned for it.*

SALERIO *That's certain, if the devil may be her judge.*

SHYLOCK *My own flesh and blood rebel!*

SOLANIO *Out upon it, old* **carrion***! Rebels it at these years?*

SHYLOCK *I say my daughter is my flesh and my blood.*

SALERIO *There is more difference between thy flesh and hers than between* **jet** *and* **ivory,** *more between your bloods than there is between red wine and* **Rhenish.** *But tell us, do you hear whether Antonio have had any loss at sea or no?*

SHYLOCK *There I have another bad match! A* **bankrout,** *a* **prodigal,** *who dare scarce show his head on the Rialto, a beggar that was used to come so* **smug** *upon the* **mart***! Let him look to his* **bond.** *He was* **wont** *to call me* **usurer.** *Let him look to his bond. He was wont to lend money for a Christian* **cursy.** *Let him look to his bond.*

SALERIO *Why, I am sure if he forfeit thou wilt not take his flesh. What's that good for?*

SHYLOCK *To bait fish withal. If it will feed nothing else, it will feed my revenge. He hath disgraced me and* **hind'red** *me half a million, laughed at my losses, mocked at my gains, scorned my nation,* **thwarted** *my bargains, cooled my friends, heated mine enemies—and what's his reason? I am a Jew. Hath not a Jew eyes? Hath not a Jew hands, organs,* **dimensions,** *senses, affections, passions?—fed with the same food, hurt with the same weapons, subject to the same diseases, healed by the same means, warmed and cooled by the same winter and summer as a Christian is? If you prick us, do we not bleed? If you tickle us, do we not laugh? If you poison us, do we not die? And if you wrong us, shall we not revenge? If we are like you in the rest, we will resemble you in that. If a Jew wrong a Christian, what is his humility? Revenge. If a Christian wrong a Jew, what should his* **sufferance** *be by Christian example? Why revenge! The* **villainy** *you teach me I will execute, and it shall go hard but I will better the instruction.*

An illustration of Shylock demanding his pound of flesh, from William Shakespeare's play *The Merchant of Venice*.

Enter a Man from Antonio.

MAN *Gentlemen, my master Antonio is at his house and desires to speak with you both.*

SALERIO *We have been up and down to seek him.*

Enter Tubal.

SOLANIO Here comes another of the tribe. A third cannot be matched, unless the devil himself turn Jew.

Exeunt [Solanio, Salerio, and Man].

SHYLOCK How now, Tubal! What news from Genoa? Hast thou found my daughter?

TUBAL I often came where I did hear of her, but cannot find her.

*SHYLOCK Why there, there, there, there! A diamond gone cost me two thousand **ducats** in **Frankford**! The curse never fell upon our nation till now; I never felt it till now. Two thousand ducats in that, and other precious, precious jewels. I would my daughter were dead at my foot, and the jewels in her ear! Would she were **hearsed** at my foot, and the ducats in her coffin! No news of them, why so?—and I know not what's spent in the search. Why thou loss upon loss! The thief gone with so much, and so much to find the thief!—and no satisfaction, no revenge! Nor no ill luck stirring but what lights o' my shoulders, no sighs but o' my breathing, no tears but o' my shedding.*

TUBAL Yes, other men have ill luck too. Antonio, as I heard in Genoa—

SHYLOCK What, what, what? Ill luck, ill luck?

*TUBAL Hath an **argosy** cast away coming from **Tripolis.***

SHYLOCK I thank God, I thank God! Is it true? is it true?

TUBAL I spoke with some of the sailors that escaped the wrack.

SHYLOCK I thank thee, good Tubal. Good news, good news! Ha, ha! Heard in Genoa?

*TUBAL Your daughter spent in Genoa, as I heard, one night **fourscore** ducats.*

SHYLOCK Thou stick'st a dagger in me. I shall never see my gold again. Fourscore ducats at a sitting, fourscore ducats!

*TUBAL There came **divers** of Antonio's creditors in my company to Venice that swear he cannot choose but break.*

SHYLOCK I am very glad of it. I'll plague him; I'll torture him. I am glad of it.

TUBAL One of them showed me a ring that he had of your daughter for a monkey.

Ducats Italian coins.

Frankford: Frankfort, Germany.

Hearsed: Placed in a coffin.

Argosy: Merchant ship.

Tripolis: Tripolitania; former province in northwest Libya.

Fourscore: Four times twenty; eighty.

Divers: Various.

SHYLOCK Out upon her! Thou torturest me, Tubal. It was my **turquoise;** I had it of Leah [his wife] when I was a bachelor. I would not have given it for a wilderness of monkeys.

TUBAL But Antonio is certainly undone.

SHYLOCK Nay, that's true, that's very true. Go, Tubal, fee me an officer; bespeak him a **fortnight** before. I will have the heart of him if he forfeit, for were he out of Venice I can make what merchandise I will. Go, Tubal, and meet me at our **synagogue;** go, good Tubal; at our synagogue, Tubal.

What happened next...

Bassanio confesses his love to Portia, who tells him to choose the proper chest. He selects the leaden one, which contains a portrait of Portia and a note permitting him to marry her. Bassanio then learns that all of Antonio's ships have been lost and he has been jailed for bankruptcy. Bassanio tells Portia of the contract with Shylock. She gives Bassanio six thousands ducats, twice the amount owed to Shylock, to free Antonio. She tells him to return home quickly before they are to be married. Meanwhile Shylock visits Antonio in jail and refuses to listen to his pleas. Shylock again emphasizes that he will "have his bond" and will not agree to a compromise.

Antonio and Shylock then appear before the Duke of Venice to plead their cases. The Duke tells Shylock to show mercy on Antonio and not insist on collecting his bond. Shylock argues that it is not up to the court to determine if the bond is fair, nor is it up to the court to decide if he, Shylock, is cruel. Shylock argues that Antonio made the agreement and should he held to it, or else the laws of Venice mean nothing. As the duke, Antonio, and Shylock argue, Portia arrives at the court. She demands that Shylock be merciful. Shylock continues to argue that he has an agreement that must be honored, even if Portia offers him three times the money he is owed. Portia is allowed to act as a judge, and she agrees that Shylock is owed the bond. Shylock rejoices and prepares to take flesh from Antonio. Portia asks Shylock if he has a sur-

Turquoise: Bluish-green mineral used for jewelry.

Fortnight: A period of two weeks.

Synagogue: Jewish house of worship.

William Shakespeare's *The Merchant of Venice* was similar to English playwright Christopher Marlowe's play *The Jew of Malta*.

geon nearby to stop the bleeding, for the bond does not say that Shylock may kill Antonio. She then adds that if Shylock spills one drop of Christian blood, he will lose not only the bond but also his entire estate.

Shylock now realizes that he cannot get his bond, so he asks for the nine thousand ducats in place of the flesh. Portia refuses, saying that Shylock wanted his bond when he thought he could cut a pound of flesh from Antonio, and should be made to honor it now even though he cannot take the flesh. She tells him to cut without spilling blood and to take exactly one pound, for any less or any more would violate the contract. Shylock asks for the three thousand ducats he loaned Antonio. Bassanio is prepared to pay but Portia stops him. Portia tells Shylock he is subject to Venetian law because he planned to take the life of a Venetian citizen. Half of his money therefore goes to Antonio, and the other half goes to the state. Shylock is to be killed. His only chance for survival is to beg mercy from the duke. The duke automatically spares his life, but Shylock asks the duke to kill him, saying that it is better to be dead than bankrupt. Antonio offers a compromise, saying he will not take half of Shylock's estate on two conditions: first, Shylock must convert to Christianity, and, second, upon his death his money goes to Lorenzo and Jessica, who have been secretly married. Shylock agrees to both conditions. According to most scholars Shakespeare uses this scene, which is Shylock's final appearance in the play, as a way to show the triumph of Christian law over Jewish law.

Did you know...

- Most Christians during the Renaissance period knew little about the Jewish religion. Many thought Jews had horns on their heads, claiming that Jewish men wore the skullcap called a yarmulke in synagogue to cover up the horns. Others continued to believe in the blood libel and thought that Jews practiced human sacrifice. Shylock's demand for a pound of flesh from Antonio capitalizes on this belief.

- In 1589, seven years before the first performance of *The Merchant of Venice,* the English playwright Christopher Marlowe wrote *The Jew of Malta.* This play features a Jewish merchant named Barabas, who is unjustly persecuted by Christians. As the play progresses, however, Barabas becomes obsessed by his desire for gold and he turns into a stereotype of the greedy Jew like Shylock. Barabas murders his daughter and an entire convent of nuns (Catholic women who devote their lives to the church) by feeding them poisoned porridge. After committing other atrocities, he himself meets a horrible fate by falling into a boiling caldron (large pot).

For More Information

Books

Dobson, Michael, and Stanley Wells, eds. *The Oxford Companion to Shakespeare,* New York: Oxford University Press, 2001.

Dommermuth-Costa, Carol. *William Shakespeare.* Minneapolis: Lerner Publications Co., 2002.

Garfield, Leon. *Shakespeare Stories II.* Boston: Houghton Mifflin Co., 1995.

Shakespeare, William. *The Merchant of Venice.* Edited by Brents Stirling. New York: Penguin Books, 1987.

Shakespeare, William. *The Riverside Shakespeare.* Edited by G. Blakemore Evans and J. M. M. Tobin. New York: Houghton Mifflin, 1997.

Thrasher, Thomas. *William Shakespeare.* San Diego, Calif.: Lucent Books, 1999.

Web Sites

"Shakespeare, William." *The Annex.* [Online] Available http://web.uvic.ca/shakespeare/Annex, April 10, 2002.

"Shakespeare, William." *MSN Encarta.* [Online] Available http://encarta.msn.com/find/Concise.asp?z=1&pg=2&ti=761562101, April 10, 2002.

The Shakespearean Homework Helper. [Online] Available http://hometown.aol.com/liadona2/shakespeare.html, April 10, 2002.

Margaret of Navarre

Excerpt from Heptaméron *(1558)*

Translated by Arthur Machen
Published in 1905

Heptaméron is considered one of the great prose works of the French Renaissance. (The Renaissance was a transition period in European history from medieval to modern times, marked by a revival of classical culture, which brought innovations in the arts and literature and initiated modern science.) The author, Margaret of Navarre (1492–1549), duchess of Angoulême, modeled *Heptaméron* on *Decameron,* a popular book by the fourteenth-century Italian writer Giovanni Boccaccio. She herself had commissioned a French translation of *Decameron,* which appeared in 1545. Margaret was a prominent figure at the court of her brother, King Francis I (see accompanying box). It was at court that she was joined by Catherine de Médicis, wife of Francis's son Henry (the future King Henry II), and others in conceiving of the idea of a French version of *Decameron.* The result was *Heptaméron,* a collection of seventy-two short stories that take place over seven days, with ten stories on each day. Two tales are told on an eighth day. Margaret had planned to write one hundred stories, as in *Decameron,* but she died before she completed the manuscript. *Heptaméron* was published in 1558.

Margaret of Navarre

Margaret of Navarre, duchess of Angoulême, was born at Cognac, France, in 1492. She was the daughter of Charles de Valois, count of Angoulême, and Louise of Savoy. Her father was a cousin of the king of France, Louis XII. Margaret and her brother Francis, the future King Francis I of France, were brought up at Cognac by their mother, who supervised their education. In 1507 Margaret and Francis left their mother's household to live at the court of Louis XII. When Francis took the throne eight years later Margaret became an important political and social figure. In 1527, two years after the death of her first husband, Margaret married Henry II, king of Navarre.

Margaret set the intellectual and cultural tone at court, especially in the 1530s and early 1540s. Interested in religious and philosophical matters, she read the Bible (the Christian holy book) and the works of Italian poets Dante and Petrarch. She was a prolific writer and produced many works, though few were published during her lifetime. In 1531 she published the long poem *Le miroir de l'âme pécheresse* (Mirror of the sinful soul), which was followed two years later by *Dialogue en forme de vision nocturne* (Dialogue in the form of a nocturnal vision). In 1547 she published a collection of her poetry under the title *Les marguerites de la marguerite des princesses.* (Pearls from the pearl of princesses; "marguerite" means both "pearl" and "daisy.") Margaret's most famous work is *Heptaméron,* which was published in 1558, nine years after her death.

Heptaméron draws moral lessons

The characters in *Heptaméron* are ten French aristocrats—five men and five women—who are stranded by a flood in the Pyrenees, a mountain range between France and Spain. They take refuge at an abbey (church of a monastery) and decide to tell stories while waiting for a bridge to be built. After each story, they comment on the tale just told, drawing from it moral lessons that usually present contradictions and have no neat conclusions. Complex relationships are established among the speakers. They focus on the difficulties of meeting the demands of a worldly life while trying to live according to the Christian message of charity.

A knight (nobleman warrior) named Simontault begins the narrative on the first day with a tale about "the bad turns done by women to men, and by men to women." The story has a complicated plot revolving around the "misdeeds"

Margaret of Navarre, duchess of Angoulême, and author of *Heptaméron*.
©*Archivo Iconografico, S.A./Corbis. Reproduced by permission of Corbis Corporation.*

of the beautiful wife—who is not given a name—of Saint Aignan, a proctor, or clergyman, in the town of Alençon. The woman has two lovers. The first is the Bishop of Séez, who heads the district where her husband's church is located. Saint Aignan approves of this relationship because the bishop gives her money. The woman's other lover is her favorite, Du Mesnil, the handsome young son of Alençon's lieutenant-general. Saint Aignan does not know about Du Mesnil. "And this fashion of life lasted a long while," Simontault says, "she having the Bishop for profit, and Du Mesnil for pleasure...." Du Mesnil does not know the woman is having an affair with the bishop, however, so he is shocked when he discovers them together. Desperate to hide her affair with Du Mesnil, the woman tells the bishop and Saint Aignan that Du Mesnil has been trying to "lay assault to her honour."

Saint Aignan hires a man to kill Du Mesnil and has the body burned. Saint Aignan soon realizes he will be charged with the crime, so he flees with his wife to England.

The following excerpt from *Heptaméron* opens near the end of the first tale, while Saint Aignan and his wife are in England.

Things to Remember While Reading an Excerpt from *Heptaméron:*

- In their absence Saint Aignan and his wife are found guilty of murder. They are ordered to pay a fine to Du Mesnil's father, and their property is seized. They return to France in disguise after Saint Aignan manages to have himself declared dead in that country. Saint Aignan then hires a wizard, or magician, named Gallery to help him escape paying the fine. Saint Aignan's wife overhears

Gallery saying that he will make wax images of five people upon whom he will cast spells—three who are to die and two with whom Saint Aignan will gain favor. When she realizes she is one of those marked for death, she reveals the plot. As a result, Saint Aignan and Gallery are put on trial. The court has mercy on them, however, because they were manipulated by Saint Aignan's wife and they are not put to death. The wife continues to sin, meeting a just fate by dying a miserable death.

- At the conclusion of the tale Simontault challenges an aged widow, Mistress Oisille, to tell a story about a virtuous woman, if one can be found. Oisille gladly takes the challenge and begins the second tale.

Excerpt from Heptaméron

*Judgment went by **default**, they [St. Aignan and his wife] were condemned to death, to pay fifteen hundred **crowns** to the father of the murdered man, and the rest of their goods were **escheated to the crown**. St. Aignan, seeing that though he was living in England, in France the law accounted him dead, accomplished so much by his services to some great lords, and by the favour of the kinsfolk of his wife, that the King of England **entreated** the King of France to grant him free pardon, and to restore to him his goods and his offices. But the King of France being assured of the enormity of his crime, sent the case to the King of England, asking him if such a deed deserved pardon, and saying that to the Duke of Alençon alone it **pertained** to grant pardon for offences done in his **duchy**. But for all these excuses he could not satisfy the King of England, who so earnestly entreated him that at last the proctor gained what he desired and returned to his home. And there, to fill up the measure of his wickedness, he called to him a wizard, named Gallery, hoping by this means to escape the paying of the fifteen hundred crowns to the father of the dead man.*

*And to this end, he and his wife with him, went up to Paris in disguise. And she, perceiving him **closeted** for a long while with the enchanter Gallery, and not being told the reason of this, on one morning played the spy and saw Gallery showing to him five*

Default: Failure to appear at a legal proceeding.

Crowns: An amount of money.

Escheated to the crown: Given back to the king.

Entreated: Asked.

Pertained: Was the duty of.

Duchy: Territory ruled by a duke.

Closeted: Closed way.

wooden images, of which three had their hands hanging down, and of the two others the hands were raised. And she heard the wizard: "We must have images made of wax like these, and they that have the hands drooping shall be made in the likeness of those that are to die, but they that have the hands uplifted shall be made in the likeness of those whose love and favour we desire." To whom the proctor: "This one shall be for the King whose grace I would gain, and this for my Lord Brinon, the chancellor of Alençon." And Gallery said to him, "We must lay these images beneath the **altar**, where they may hear **mass**, together with the words that you shall presently say after me." And speaking of them that had the drooping arms, the proctor said that one should be Master Gilles du Mesnil, father of him who was murdered, for he knew that as long as he was alive he would not cease from pursuing him. And another, that was made in the likeness of a woman, should be for my lady the Duchess of Alençon, the sister of the King; since so well did she love Du Mesnil, her old servant, and had so great a knowledge of the proctor's wickedness in other matters, that unless she died, he could not live. And the last image, that was also made in the likeness of a woman, should be his wife, since she was the beginning of all his **evil hap,** and he knew that she would never **amend** the wickedness of her ways. But when this wife of his, who saw through a **chink** in the door all that was done, heard that she was numbered among the dead, it was her **humour** to send her husband before her. And pretending to go and borrow money of an uncle of hers, named Neaufle, Master of Requests to the Duke of Alençon, she told him of her husband, and all that she had seen and heard him do. This Neaufle aforesaid, like a good old servant, went forthwith to the chancellor of the Duchy of Alençon, and showed him the whole of the matter. And since the Duke and Duchess chanced not to be at court on that day, the chancellor went and told this strange case to the Regent, mother of the King and of the Duchess, who straightway sought out La Barre, Provost of Paris; and such good **diligence** did he make that he **clapped up** the proctor and his wizard Gallery, who confessed freely the crime, without being put to the question, or in any way **constrained.** And the matter of their accusation was made out and brought to the King, whereupon some, willing to save the lives of these men, would **fain** persuade him that by their enchantments they sought nothing but his grace. But the King, being as tender of his sister's life as of his own, commanded that sentence should be given as if they had attempted his own **peculiar** person. Nevertheless, the Duchess of Alençon made **entreaty**

Altar: Center of worship.

Mass: Catholic worship service.

Evil hap: Misfortune.

Amend: Change.

Chink: A narrow crack or opening.

Humour: Impulse.

Diligence: Earnest and persistent effort.

Clapped up: Arrested.

Constrained: Restricted.

Fain: Willingly.

Peculiar: Distinctive.

Entreaty: A plea.

A scene from Giovanni Boccaccio's work *Decameron*. Margaret of Navarre modeled her work *Heptaméron* on *Decameron*. ©Archivo Iconografico, S. A./Corbis. Reproduced by permission of Corbis Corporation.

for the life of this proctor, and for the doom of death to be changed to some other punishment. So this was granted her, and the proctor, together with the wizard, were sent to the galleys of St. Blancart at Marseilles, where they ended their days in close imprisonment, having time wherein to consider their sins, how great they had been. And the wife, when her husband was removed, sinned more wickedly than before, and so died miserably.

[Simontault concludes] I entreat you, ladies, consider well the evil that cometh of a wicked woman, and how many mishaps proceeded from the sin of this one I have told you of. You will find that from the time Eve made Adam to sin, all women have been for the torturing, killing, and damnation of men. As for me, such an experience have I of their cruelty that I am well assured that when I meet with death and damnation, it will be through despair of her whom I love. Yet so **besotted** am I, that I must needs confess that this hell delights me more coming from her hand than would heaven from the hand of another." Parlamente [one of the five noblewomen], **feigning** not to understand that it was of her that he made this **discourse**, said to

Besotted: Made stupid.

Feigning: Pretending.

Discourse: Statement.

him: "Since this hell of yours is as pleasant as you say, it skills not to fear the devil who sends it." But **wrathfully** he replied to her: "If my devil should become visible as black as it has made me unhappy, this company would be struck with as great fear as my delight is in regarding it, but the fire of my love makes me to forget the fire of my hell. So to speak no more of this matter, I will give my vote to Mistress Oisille to tell the second novel, and sure am I, that if she would tell that she knows of women, she would be of my opinion." Instantly the company turned toward her, praying her to make a beginning. To this she agreed, and smiling began thus:

It seems to me, ladies, that he who has given his vote to me has made such an ill report of women by this true story of a woman who was exceedingly wicked, that I shall have to call to mind all these old years of mine, to find one woman whose virtue shall give the lie to his judgment. And since there is come into my mind the recollection of a woman well worthy of being had in everlasting remembrance, I will tell you her history.

What happened next...

Because of the frank and stark depiction of sexual desire, many sixteenth-century readers were perplexed by the book and tended to view it as a collection of indecent tales. Late-twentieth-century scholars reevaluated *Heptaméron,* however, stressing its complex narrative and the prominence of women in the tales. The book is now considered a classic of the French Renaissance.

Did you know...

• Since the publication of *Heptaméron* in 1558, there has been a dispute about the actual author of the tales. A nineteenth-century scholar, Charles Nodier, claimed that most or all of the stories were written by Bonaventure de Périers, an attendant in Margaret of Navarre's court. No evidence has been found to support this theory, but twentieth-century scholars concluded that *Heptaméron* probably had sev-

Wrathfully: Angrily.

eral authors instead of only one. The tales may have been told to Margaret by her court attendants. This is the view reported by a man named Brantôme, who was the grandson of one of her ladies-in-waiting. According to Brantôme, his grandmother said Margaret heard the stories and wrote them down while she was being carried around the country in a litter by her servants. (A litter is a covered and curtained couch with long handles called shafts used for carrying a single passenger.)

- Margaret of Navarre was an early supporter of reform in the Roman Catholic Church. She remained outwardly obedient to Catholicism, but she protected leading French reformers such as Guillaume Briçonnet and Jacques d'ètaples Lefèvre. They were suspected of advocating Lutheranism. Lutheranism was a religious reform movement led by the German priest Martin Luther, which later resulted in the Protestant Reformation and the formation of a Christian religion that is separate from Roman Catholicism (see **Martin Luther** entry). Margaret's poems *Mirror of the sinful soul* and *Dialogue in the form of a nocturnal vision* were condemned by the theology faculty (professors of religion) at the Sorbonne, a college in Paris, because of the reformist views she expressed in them.

For More Information

Books

Machen, Arthur, trans. *The Heptaméron, or Tales and Novels of Marguerite, Queen of Navarre*. New York: E. F. Dutton, 1905.

Marguerite de Navarre. *The Heptaméron*. Translated by Paul A. Chilton. New York: Penguin Books, 1984.

Web Sites

The Heptameron of Margaret, Queen of Navarre. [Online] Available http://digital.library.upenn.edu/women/navarre/heptameron/heptameron.html, April 10, 2002.

"Margaret of Angoulême." *Britannica.com*. [Online] Available http://www.britannica.com/seo/m/margaret-of-angouleme, April 10, 2002.

"Margaret of Navarre." *Infoplease.com*. [Online] Available http://www.infoplease.com/ce6/people/A0831778.html, April 10, 2002.

Miguel de Cervantes

Excerpts from Don Quixote *(1605)*
Translated by Burton Raffel
Published in 1999

Don Quixote (*Quijote* in Spanish) is considered one of the great masterpieces of world literature. This work was largely responsible for creating what is known as the modern novel. (A novel is a long narrative work that features fictional, or imaginary, characters involved in complex plots.) *Don Quixote* has been translated into more than sixty languages and its central character, Don Quixote of la Mancha, has become a major figure in Western (non-Asian) culture. Don Quixote's image has been popularized in films, musicals, and paintings. His creator, Miguel de Cervantes (1547–1616), lived at the end of the glorious years of the Spanish empire and fought heroically at the decisive sea battle of Lepanto. However, throughout his life Cervantes lived on the margins of society in a continuous struggle for survival. On occasion he was subjected to all the mishaps of Don Quixote, with extended periods in captivity and ceaseless economic hardship. These experiences are reflected in the novel's narrative, which is sympathetic and touchingly humane.

 Don Quixote contains a number of the popular literary styles and subjects of the Renaissance, such as the romantic novel that focuses on tales of chivalry and issues of religion and faith. (The Renaissance was a cultural revolution that began in Italy in the mid-1300s. It was initiated by scholars called humanists who promoted the human-centered values of ancient Greece and Rome. Humanist ideals were soon influencing the arts, literature, philosophy, science, religion, and politics in Italy and later into the rest of Europe.) Chivalry was a medieval tradition that required knights, or nobleman soldiers, to pledge themselves to a complex code of honor. Knights frequently dedicated their military adventures to ladies, whose virtue they vowed to protect. Cervantes originally intended to mock the popular chivalric romances and the adventures stories of errant, or traveling, knights. He created the character of Don Quixote, an elderly gentleman who is driven insane by his passion for reading chivalric romances. Don Quixote leaves

his home, having decided to revive heroic times by reenacting knightly feats. Later, with the promise of fabulous rewards, he convinces the poor peasant, Sancho Panza, to be his squire, or shield bearer. The novel narrates the absurd adventures of the knight and squire as they travel through Spain. Using a satiric approach, Cervantes depicted characters who reflected their society, thus making a commentary on the social customs of the day. (Satire is criticism through the use of humor.)

Miguel de Cervantes, author of *Don Quixote,* was largely responsible for creating what has become known as the modern novel.

Things to Remember While Reading Excerpts from *Don Quixote:*

• The first excerpt comes at the end of chapter one, where Don Quixote embarks on his first quest as a errant knight. After assembling his armor (metal suit worn in battle), he selects and names his horse, adopts a noble-sounding name for himself, and chooses the name for the lady to whom he will dedicate his quest.

Miguel de Cervantes

Miguel de Cervantes Saavedra (known as Cervantes) was born in 1547 in Alcalá de Henares, Spain. He was the fourth of seven children in the family of Rodrigo de Cervantes, a barber-surgeon, and Leonor de Cortina. Cervantes never attended a university, and any knowledge he acquired over the years was due to his life-long devotion to independent reading. In 1570 he joined the Spanish army in Italy. The following year he was wounded at the Battle of Lepanto, the famous naval conflict in which the Christian fleet (combined naval forces of European nations) defeated the Turkish fleet off the coast of Greece. Cervantes remained in Italy as a soldier until 1575, when he decided to return to Spain. During the voyage three Turkish galleys intercepted his ship off the coast of Marseille, France. The crew and passengers were taken as captives to Algiers, Africa. Cervantes's ransom (money paid in exchange for release) was set impossibly high, so he spent the next five years in prison. He made several failed escape attempts. In 1580 Cervantes's family finally secured his freedom by paying the ransom of five hundred escudos (an amount of Spanish money).

Upon returning to Spain in 1581 Cervantes had difficulty finding work. At one point he tried to immigrate to the Americas, but was denied official permis-

- In the second excerpt, from the end of chapter seven, Don Quixote is preparing for his second quest. By this time he has had several misadventures, and he concludes that he might avoid such mishaps in the future if he is accompanied by a squire (knight's assistant). All the great knights, who he has been reading about, traveled with squires who carried the knights' shields and other equipment and aided them in battle. Don Quixote therefore vows to become a proper knight, and he sets out to find his squire. He chooses a local farmer, Sancho Panza.

- The third excerpt, from the opening of chapter eight, is one of the most memorable scenes in world literature. Against the common-sense warnings of Sancho Panza, Don Quixote attacks windmills that he mistakenly believes to be evil giants. This scene is the source of the familiar expression "tilting at windmills," which is used

sion. During this time he wrote his first novel, *La Galatea* (1585), which brought him prestige but little economic security. In 1584 he married Catalina de Salazar y Palacios, a woman eighteen years his junior. The previous year Cervantes had fathered an illegitimate daughter, Isabel de Saavedra, who was his only offspring. He did not acknowledge her until she was fifteen. In 1587 he was appointed commissary (officer in charge of supplies) for the Spanish Armada. Cervantes was later accused of mismanagement and was held in Spanish prisons in 1592 and 1597. Possibly during his last imprisonment Cervantes conceived the idea of writing *Don Quixote*. The novel was published in 1605 to great acclaim. When another man attempted to write an unauthorized sequel, Cervantes decided to write the second part of *Don Quixote*. It was published in 1615. Three years earlier Cervantes had released *The Exemplary Novels*. In the prologue (introduction) he claimed to be the first person ever to write novellas (short stories in a form that originated in Italy) in Spanish. Before his death in 1616 he was working on another novel, *Los trabajos de Persiles y Segismunda* (The Labors of Persiles and Segismunda). Cervantes was buried in an unmarked grave at a convent in Madrid. His wife survived him by ten years, and his daughter died in 1662.

when referring to a foolhardy venture that is sure to end in failure or disappointment.

Excerpts from Don Quixote

Chapter One

*The first thing he did was polish up his great-grandfather's suit of armor, which for a century or so had been lying, thrown in a corner and forgotten, covered with mildew and quietly rusting away. He got it as clean and bright as he could, but saw that it had a major deficiency: the helmet was gone, and all that was left was a metal headpiece that would cover just the top of his skull. So he put together, **ingeniously,** a kind of half-helmet of cardboard that, fitted into the*

Ingeniously: Cleverly.

headpiece, looked very much like the real thing. True, when he want-ed to test its strength and see if it could stand up under a slashing stroke, he pulled out his sword and gave it a couple of whacks, and the very first blow undid in a second what had taken him a week to put together. He couldn't help but think it a poor sign that he'd de-stroyed it so easily, so to safeguard himself against that risk he went back to work, lining the inside with iron bars until he was satisfied it was strong enough, after which, not wanting to make any further ex-periments, he declared it a perfect, finished helmet, ready for use.

Then he went to have a look at his skinny old horse, whose hide had more cracks than a clipped coin.... He spent four days trying to decide what name to give the old horse, because—as he said to himself—it would be wrong for the steed of such a celebrated knight, a horse with such merit of its own, not to bear a famous name. What he was after was something to make clear what the animal had been before his master turned to knighthood, and what it had now become. It was clear to him that, the master having changed his state, the horse's name had to reflect the new condition of things—had to be something great and famous, in order to prop-erly indicate the new way of life, the new profession, that the horse had too adopted. After he'd proposed and discarded a huge list of names, wiping out each one, framing another, then getting rid of that one too, dipping over and over again into his memory and his imagination, he finally decided to call the animal Rocinante *[rocin = old horse; ante = before], which struck him as a truly lofty name, resonant, and also meaningful, because an old horse was exactly what it had been before, while now it had risen to be first and fore-most among all the old horses in the world.*

Having settled on such a fine name for his horse, he turned to himself, and spent eight more days thinking until at last he decided to call himself Don Quijote *[quijote = thigh armor]—a plain fact which, as we have said, persuades the authors of this highly **vera-cious** history that, beyond any question, his family name must have been Quijada, rather than Quesada, as others have claimed. Yet re-membering that the brave Amadís was not content to call himself just plain Amadís, but added on his kingdom's name, in order to make it famous, too, thus terming himself Amadís of Gaul, so as a good knight he wanted to add his region's name to his own and fi-nally decided to **dub** himself* Don Quijote of La Mancha, *which as far as he was concerned neatly explained his **lineage** and his ori-gins, both of which he thus honored.*

Veracious: Truthful.

Dub: Name.

Lineage: Family line.

Well, with his armor scrubbed clean, and his helmet ready, and then his horse **christened** and himself confirmed, he realized that all he needed and had to hunt for was a lady to be in love with, since a knight errant without love entanglements would be like a tree without leaves or fruit, or a body without a soul. So he said to himself:

"Now, if for my sins, or by good fortune, I happen to find a giant right here in this neighborhood, which after all is something that usually happens to knights errant, and we have a go at it and I overthrow him, or maybe split him right down the middle, or, however it happens, conquer and utterly defeat him, wouldn't it be a good idea to have someone to whom I could send him, so he could go and kneel down in front of my sweet lady and say, his voice humble and **submissive,** 'I, my lady, am the giant Caraculiambro, lord of the island of Malindrania, defeated in man-to-man combat by that knight who can never be too much praised, Don Quijote de La Mancha, who has sent me here to offer myself at your pleasure, to be dealt with however your Grace may happen to think best'?"

Oh, how our good knight relished the delivery of this speech, especially once he'd decided who was going to be his lady love! It turns out, according to some people, that not too far from where he lived there was a very pretty peasant girl, with whom he was supposed, once upon a time, to have been in love, although (as the story goes) she never knew it nor did he ever say a word to her. Her name was Aldonza Lorenzo, and he thought it a fine idea to bestow on her the title of Mistress of his Thoughts. Hunting for a name as good as the one he'd given himself, a name that would be appropriate for that princess and noble lady, he decided to call her Dulcinea del Toboso [toboso = limestone rock], since Toboso was where she came from. To him it seemed a singularly musical name, rare, full of meaning, like all the others he'd assigned to himself and everything that belonged to him.

Chapter Seven

During this time, too, Don Quijote sought out a farmer, a neighbor of his and a good man (if we can use that term for anyone who's poor) but not very well **endowed** from the neck up. To make a long story short, he piled so many words on him, coaxing him, making him promises, that the poor fellow agreed to ride out with him and serve as his squire. Among other things, Don Quijote told him he ought to be delighted to join the quest because you could never tell when an adventure might earn them, in two shakes of a lamb's tail, a whole island, and Don Quijote would leave him there to be its governor. Because of promises like this, and many more of the same sort,

Christened: Given a name.

Submissive: Obedient.

Endowed: Possessing a natural ability for something.

Don Quixote and Sancho Panza riding on their horses, a scene from Miguel de Cervantes's novel *Don Quixote*. *Reproduced by permission of Hulton Archive.*

Pawning Leaving at a pawnshop in exchange for a loan of money.

Biblical patriarch: Prophet in the Old Testament, the first part of the Bible.

Sancho Panza—which was the farmer's name—left his wife and children and agreed to become his neighbor's squire.

Don Quijote promptly set to work hunting up money and, selling something here, ***pawning*** something there, making one bad bargain after another, he managed to put together a fair-sized sum. He also wangled a small shield for himself (borrowed from a friend) and, patching up his helmet as best he could, warned his squire of the exact day and hour at which he planned to ride out, so Sancho could make sure he had everything he was going to need. And above all else Don Quijote advised him to bring along saddlebags, which Sancho said he would do, and he'd bring a very fine donkey, too, because he hadn't had much practice getting places on foot. Don Quijote had some doubts about the donkey, trying to remember if there had been a knight errant whose squire rode along on an ass, but couldn't recall a single one. In spite of which he decided to take Sancho with him, intending to arrange a more honorable mount as soon as he had the chance, by seizing a horse from the first ill-mannered knight he bumped into....One night they rode out of the village without anyone seeing them, and rode so far that, by dawn, they thought it would be impossible to find them, even if a search were made.

Sancho Panza jogged along on his donkey like some **biblical patriarch** carrying his saddlebags and his leather wine bottle, wanting very badly to see himself the governor of an island, as his master had promised. Don Quijote had decided to go in the very same direction, and along the very same road, as on his first expedition, which led through the fields of Montiel, which he crossed with less difficulty than the last time, for it was early morning and the sun's rays came slanting down and did not tire them out. Then Sancho Panza said to his master:

"Now be careful, your grace, sir knight errant, you don't forget that island you promised me, because no matter how big it is I'll know how to govern it."

To which Don Quijote answered:

*"You must know, Sancho Panza my friend, that it used to be very common, in ancient times, for knights errant to make their squires governor of whatever islands or regions they conquered, and I am resolved not to neglect this gracious—indeed, I intend to improve on it, for occasionally, and I suspect most of the time, they waited until their squires had grown old and fed up with such service, enduring bad days and even worse nights, and then gave them a title—**count,** or more often **marquis** of some valley or province, more or less. But if you and I both live, it could be that in less then a week I'll have conquered a kingdom to which others pay **allegiance,** which would be just right for crowning you ruler of one of those **subordinate domains.** Nor should you think this in any way remarkable, for no one can possibly foresee or even imagine the way the world turns for such knights, so it could easily happen that I will be able to grant you still more than my promise."*

"So," said Sancho Panza, "if I become a king, by one of those miracles your grace is talking about, at the very least my old lady, Teresa, would get to be a queen, and my kids would be princes."

"But who could possibly doubt it?" answered Don Quijote.

*"I doubt it," replied Sancho Panza, "because it seems to me that, even if God let crowns come raining down all over the earth, none would land on my wife's head. You see, señor, she wouldn't be worth two cents as a queen. She might make a better **countess,** but it wouldn't be easy even with God's help."*

*"Put yourself in God's hands, Sancho," said Don Quijote, "and He will give both you and your wife what it is best you should each have. But don't so lower your spirit that you'll be satisfied with less than a **provincial governorship.**"*

"I won't, my lord," answered Sancho, "especially since I've got a master like your grace, who understands just what's best for me and what I can handle."

Chapter Eight

—the great success won by our brave Don Quijote in his dreadful, unimaginable encounter with two windmills, plus other honorable events well worth remembering

Just then, they came upon thirty or forty windmills, which (as it happens) stand in the fields of Montiel, and as soon as Don Quijote saw them he said to his squire:

Count: Nobleman.

Marquis: Nobleman ranking below a count.

Allegiance: Loyalty.

Subordinate domains: Dependent states.

Countess: Lady; wife of a nobleman.

Provincial governorship: Position of governor of a state within a kingdom.

"Destiny guides our fortunes more favorably than we could have expected. Look there, Sancho Panza, my friend, and see those thirty or so wild giants, with whom I intend to do battle and to kill each and all of them, so with their stolen booty we can begin to enrich ourselves. This is noble, righteous warfare, for it is wonderfully useful to God to have such an evil race wiped from the face of the earth."

"What giants?" asked Sancho Panza.

"The ones you can see over there," answered his master, "with the huge arms, some of which are nearly two leagues long."

"Now look, your grace," said Sancho, "what you see over there aren't giants, but windmills, and what seem to be arms are just their sails, that go around in the wind and turn the **millstone.**"

"Obviously," replied Don Quijote, "you don't know much about adventures. Those are giants—and if you're frightened, take yourself away from here and say your prayers, while I go charging into savage and unequal combat with them."

Saying which, he spurred his horse, Rocinante, paying no attention to the shouts of Sancho Panza, his squire, warning him that without any question it was windmills and not giants he was going to attack. So utterly convinced was he they were giants, indeed, that he neither heard Sancho's cries nor noticed, close as he was, what they really were, but charged on, crying:

"Flee not, oh cowards and dastardly creatures, for he who attacks you is a knight alone and unaccompanied."

Just then the wind blew up a bit, and the great sails began to stir, which Don Quijote saw and cried out:

"Even should you shake more arms than the giant Briareus himself, you'll still have to deal with me."

As he said this, he entrusted himself with all his heart to his lady Dulcinea, imploring her to help and sustain him at such a critical moment, and then, with his shield held high and his spear braced in its socket, and Rocinante at a full gallop, he charged directly at the first windmill he came to, just as a sudden swift gust of wind sent its sail swinging hard around, smashing the spear to bits and sweeping up the knight and his horse, tumbling them all battered and bruised to the ground. Sancho Panza came rushing to his aid, as fast as his donkey could run, but when he got to his master, found him unable to move, such a blow had he been given by the falling horse.

"God help me!" said Sancho. "Didn't I tell your grace to be careful what you did, that these were just windmills, and anyone who could ignore that had to have windmills in his head?"

"Silence, Sancho, my friend," answered Don Quijote. "Even more than other things, war is subject to **perpetual** change. What's more, I think the truth is that the same Frestón the magician, who stole away my room and my books, transformed these giants into windmills, in order to deprive me of the gory of **vanquishing** them,

Millstone: Large stone used to grind grain in a mill.

Perpetual: Unending.

Vanquishing: Conquering.

so bitter is his hatred of me. But in the end, his evil tricks will have little power against my good sword."

"God's will be done," answered Sancho Panza.

*Then, helping his master to his feet, he got him back up on Rocinante, whose shoulder was half **dislocated**. After which, discussing the adventure they'd just experienced, they followed the road toward Lápice Pass, for there said Don Quijote, they couldn't fail to find adventures of all kinds, it being a well-traveled highway....*

What happened next...

The popularity of *Don Quixote* was so extraordinary that in 1614 a man named Avellaneda attempted to write a sequel without Cervantes's permission. Cervantes was so enraged that he decided to write the second part of *Don Quixote*, which was published in 1615. At the conclusion Don Quixote dies after recovering his sanity, much to the distress of a transformed Sancho, who is eager to engage in more adventures. With Don Quixote's death Cervantes ended the possibility of further adventures for his character.

Cervantes's achievements as a novelist did not guarantee him the economic security that best-sellers bring their authors today. In the seventeenth century writers lost the rights to their work after selling it to a merchant. Therefore, Cervantes had no access to the profits made from his books. Before he died in 1616, he was trying to finish what would be his last novel, *Los trabajos de Persiles y Segismunda* (The Labors of Persiles and Segismunda). The book was published by his widow after his death. Cervantes was proud of this novel and thought its success would exceed that of *Don Quixote*. *Los trabajos de Persiles y Segismunda* was not well received, however, and Cervantes's fame rests on his creation of the errant knight and his faithful squire.

Don Quixote is one of the few books in Western literature that has been translated into most languages. The literary influence of the novel has been immense. Direct traces can be identified in the work of countless other authors of various na-

Dislocated: Pulled out of place.

tionalities. In addition, thinkers and philosophers have dedicated essays to the myth of Don Quixote. Twentiethcentury musical productions, such as *The Man of La Mancha,* and movies have been inspired by *Don Quixote.* Modern artists like the Spanish painter Pablo Picasso (1881–1973) have immortalized the image of the errant knight escorted by his faithful squire.

Did you know...

- *Don Quixote* contributed many familiar expressions to the English language. A few of them are: "the sky"s the limit," "thanks for nothing," "mind your own business," "think before you speak," "forgive and forget," "to smell a rat," "turning over a new leaf," "the haves and have-nots," "born with a silver spoon in his mouth," "the pot calling the kettle black," and "you've seen nothing yet."

- Cervantes described his years of captivity in several plays, as well as in the "The captive's" stories in *Don Quixote* (chapters 39–41). In his first work of narrative prose, *Infomación de Argel* (Information of Algiers) he wrote about the four unsuccessful escape attempts he organized. The reader learns that he refused to inform on any of his fellow captives, and he described a near miraculous escape from the severe punishments usually given out for those offenses.

- In addition to writing novels, Cervantes tried to become a playwright. At that time in Madrid, theater-going was a popular form of entertainment, much like going to the movies today. There were several open-air theaters in the city, and people were eager to see new plays. Cervantes decided to try his fortune in the thriving market of comedies. His main rival was Lope de Vega, who was also the public's favorite playwright. Cervantes wrote several plays, but only two have survived: *El cerco de Numancia* and *El trato de Argel.* He eventually abandoned his attempts at a career in the theater.

For More Information

Books

Cervantes, Miguel de. *Don Quijote.* Translated by Burton Raffel. Edited by Diana de Armas Wilson. New York: Norton, 1999.

Canavaggio, Jean. *Cervantes.* Translated by J. R. Jones. New York: Norton, 1990.

Sound Recordings

Cervantes, Miguel de. *Don Quixote.* St. Paul, Minn.: HighBridge,1997.

Man of La Mancha. New York: Sony Classical, 1996.

Video Recordings

Don Quixote. TNT Original: Hallmark Entertainment Production, 2000.

Man of La Mancha. Mich.: CBS/FOX Video, 1984.

Web Sites

"Cervantes, Miguel de." *Britannica.com.* [Online] Available http://www.britannica.com/eb/article?eu=114980&tocid=0&query=cervantes, April 10, 2002.

"Cervantes Saavedra, Miguel de." *Encyclopedia.com.* [Online] Available http://www.encyclopedia.com/searchpool.asp?target=@DOCTITLE%20Cervantes%20Saavedra%20%20Miguel%20de, April 10, 2002.

The Don Quixote Exhibit. [Online] Available http://milton.mse.jhu.edu:8006/, April 10, 2002.

Michel de Montaigne

Excerpts from "Of Cannibals" (1580)
Reprinted in *Michel de Montaigne: Selected Essays*
Translated by Donald M. Frame
Published in 1943

Today the essay is a familiar literary genre (form), which appears in books, magazines, and newspapers. It is now considered an ideal mode of self-expression that enables the writer to communicate his or her inner thoughts and feelings. Yet the essay was unknown until the late Renaissance period, when it was introduced by the French author Michel de Montaigne (1533–1592). The term essay was first used by Montaigne for short prose discussions. It comes from the French word *essai,* meaning "trial," "an attempt," or "testing." The informal essay as Montaigne understood and developed it is the method a writer uses to test his or her own views on life and the self.

"What do I know?"

In 1580 Montaigne published *Essais* (Essays), a collection of his essays, in which he used self-portrayal as a method for reaching conclusions about human experience in general. He was not a systematic thinker, however, and he did not maintain a single point of view. Instead, he preferred to show the randomness of his own thought as representative of the

French author Michel de Montaigne introduced the literary genre of the essay. *Photograph courtesy of The Library of Congress.*

self-contradiction to which all people are prone. Montaigne's characteristic motto was "Que sais-je?" ("What do I know?") Although he was skeptical about the power of human reason, he argued that each person should have self-knowledge in order to live happily.

Since Montaigne believed that "each man bears the complete stamp of the human condition," his essays can also be seen as portraits of humankind in all its diversity. He constantly attacked the presumption, arrogance, and pride of ordinary people, yet he held the highest view of human dignity. As a skeptic (one who maintains an attitude of doubt), Montaigne opposed intolerance and fanaticism, saying that truth is never one-sided. He championed individual freedom but held that even repressive laws should be obeyed. He feared violence and anarchy (lawlessness or political disorder) and was suspicious of any radical proposals that might jeopardize the existing order. Acceptance and detachment were for him the keys to happiness.

Montaigne wrote on a wide range of subjects, including idleness, the education of children, friendship, solitude, the inconsistency of human actions, and vanity. Excerpts from one of his best-known essays, "Of Cannibals," are reprinted below.

Things to Remember While Reading Excerpts from "Of Cannibals":

• In "Of Cannibals" Montaigne contemplated a society of cannibals (people who eat other humans) that had been recently discovered in Antarctic France (Brazil). His purpose was to draw comparisons between supposedly "civilized" French society and "barbarians" (those who have no culture or religion).

Michel de Montaigne

Michel de Montaigne was born in 1533 into a noble, or aristocratic, family in Périgord near Bordeaux, France. His father, Pierre Eyquem, was a merchant and municipal, or city, official whose grandfather was the first nobleman of the line. His mother, Antoinette de Louppes (Lopez), was descended from Spanish Jews, called Marranos, who had converted to Catholicism. Montaigne was educated at the Collège de Guyenne, in Bordeaux. In 1557 he obtained the position of councilor in the Bordeaux Parlement, where he met his closest friend, étienne de La Boétie (1530– 1563). La Boétie died from dysentery (infectious disease causing extreme diarrhea) in 1563. The loss of his friend was a serious emotional blow that Montaigne later described in his essay "On Friendship."

In 1568, after his father died, Montaigne inherited the rank of lord. Before his death, Pierre Montaigne had persuaded his son to translate into French the *Book of Creatures or Natural Theology* by the fifteenth-century Spanish theologian Raymond of Sabunde (died 1436). The work was an *apologia,* or apology, for the Christian religion based on proofs from the natural world, which he published in 1569. Montaigne later based the longest of his many essays, "The Apology for Raymond Sebond," on this translation.

In 1570 Montaigne resigned from the Bordeaux Parlement and retired to his country estate, where he began writing *Essais.* Ten years later books One and Two were published in Bordeaux. From 1580 until 1584 Montaigne served as mayor of Bordeaux, and he indirectly defended his regime in the essay "Of Husbanding Your Will." He was in failing health during his last years, so a young admirer, Marie de Gournay (1565–1645), worked on the expanded edition of his works. Drawing mainly from notes made by Montaigne, Gournay published the edition in 1595, three years after his death. It was the basis of the first English-language edition by John Florio, which was published in 1603.

- "Of Cannibals" is a lengthy essay, in which Montaigne gave a detailed account of the cannibals' society. He described their houses, daily life, religious customs, relations between men and women, child-rearing practices, music, food, and other aspects of the culture. He relied on evidence provided by a man he mentions in the opening excerpt, who had lived among the cannibals for ten or twelve years. Montaigne had personally tasted a drink that was popular among the cannibals, and he had heard a song and some poetry. He also interviewed a native of the society who visited France.

- On the basis of his own observations, Montaigne concluded that "civilized" people may be no better or worse than "savages." In fact, he argued, civilization had smothered the natural instincts of human beings.

Excerpts from "Of Cannibals"

I had with me for a long time a man who had lived for ten or twelve years in that other world which was discovered in our century, in the place where Villegaignon landed, and which he called Antarctic France. This discovery of a boundless country seems worthy of consideration....

*We need a man either very honest, or so simple that he has not the stuff to build up false inventions and give them **plausibility**; and **wedded** to no theory. Such was my man; and besides this, he has at various times brought sailors and merchants, whom he had known on that trip, to see me. So I content myself with his information, without inquiring what the cosmographers say about it.*

*Now, to return to my subject, I think there is nothing barbarous and savage in this nation, from what I have been told, except that each man calls barbarism whatever is not his own practice; for indeed it seems we have no other test of truth and reason than the example and pattern of the opinions and customs of the country we live in. There is always the perfect religion, the perfect government, the perfect and accomplished usage in all things. Those people are wild, just as we call wild fruits that Nature has produced by herself and in her normal course; whereas really it is those that we have changed artificially and led astray from the common order, that we should rather call wild. In the former the genuine, most useful and natural virtues and **properties** are alive and vigorous, which we have **debased** in the latter, and have only adapted to the pleasure of our corrupted taste. And yet for all that, the **savor** and delicacy of some uncultivated fruits of those countries is quite as excellent, even to our taste, as that of our own. It is not reasonable that art should win the place of honor over our great and powerful mother Nature. We have so overloaded the beauty and richness of her works by our inventions that we have quite smothered her....*

Plausibility: Believability.

Wedded: Dependent upon.

Properties: Characteristics.

Debased: Corrupted.

Savor: Flavor.

Vexed: Puzzled.

Traffic: Exchange of communication.

Magistrate: Judge.

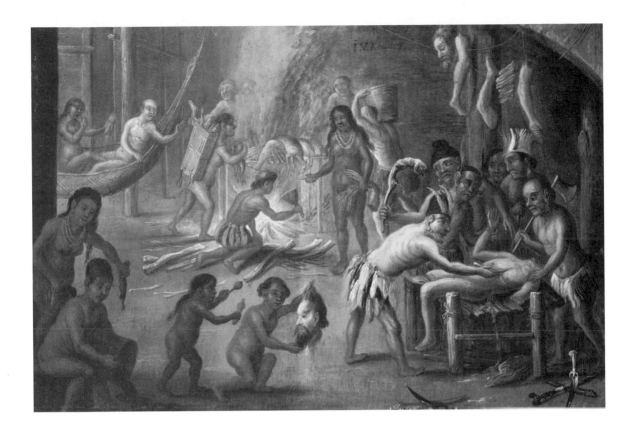

These nations, then, seem to me barbarous in this sense, that they have been fashioned very little by the human mind, and are still very close to their original naturalness. The laws of nature still rule them, very little corrupted by ours; but they are in such a state of purity that I am sometimes **vexed** that knowledge of them did not come earlier, in the days when there were men able to judge them better than we.... This is a nation ... in which there is no sort of **traffic**, no knowledge of letters, no science of numbers, no name for a **magistrate** or for political superiority, no custom of **servitude,** no riches or poverty, no contracts, no successions, no **partitions,** no occupations but leisure ones, nor care for any but common kinship, no clothes, no agriculture, no metal, no use of wine or corn. The very words that signify lying, **treachery, dissimulation, avarice,** envy, belittling, pardon, unheard of....

They have their wars with the nations beyond the mountains, further inland, to which they go quite naked, with no other **arms** than bows or wooden swords pointed at one end, in the manner of

Indians as Cannibals **by Jan van Kessel I.** *©Christie's Images/Corbis. Reproduced by permission of Corbis Corporation.*

Servitude: People being forced to serve others; slavery.

Partitions: Social divisions.

Treachery: Betrayal.

Dissimulation: Engaging in untruth.

Avarice: Greed.

Arms: Weapons.

the tongues of our **boar spears.** It is marvelous what firmness they show in their combats, which never end but in slaughter and blood-shed; for as for **routs** and terror, they do not know what that means.

Each man brings back as his trophy the head of the enemy he has killed, and sets it up at the entrance to his dwelling. After treating their prisoners well for a long time with all the hospitality they can think of, the captor of each one calls a great assembly of his acquaintances. He ties a rope to one of the prisoner's arms, by the end of which he holds him, a few steps away, for fear of being hurt, and gives his dearest friend the other arm to hold in the same way; and these two, in the presence of the whole assembly, **dispatch** him with their swords. This done, they roast him and eat him in common and send some pieces to their absent friends. This is not, as people think, for nourishment, as of old the **Scythians** used to do; it is **betoken** an extreme revenge....

I am not sorry that we notice the barbarous horror of such acts, but I am heartily sorry that, judging their faults rightly, we should be so blind to our own. I think there is more barbarity in eating a man alive than in eating him dead, in tearing by tortures and the **rack** a body still full of feeling, in roasting him bit by bit, having him bitten and mangled by dogs and swine (as we have not only read but seen within fresh memory, not among ancient enemies, but among neighbors and fellow citizens, and what is worse, on the **pretext** of **piety** and religion) than in roasting and eating him after he is dead....

Then we may well call these people barbarians, in respect to the rules of reason, but not in respect to ourselves, who surpass them in every kind of barbarity.

Their warfare is wholly noble and generous, and as excusable and beautiful as this human disease can be; its only basis among them is the jealousy of **valor.** They are not fighting for the conquest of new lands, for they still enjoy that natural abundance that provides them without toil and trouble with all necessary things in such **profusion** that they have no wish to enlarge their boundaries. They are still in that happy state of desiring only as much as their natural needs demand; anything beyond that is **superfluous** to them....

Three of these men, not knowing how much their repose and happiness will pay some day for the knowledge of the corruptions of this side of the ocean, and that of this **intercourse** will come their ruin, which I suppose is already well advanced—poor **wretches,** to have let themselves be tricked by the desire for new things, and to

Boar spears: Heavy weapons with sharp points.

Routs: Attacks.

Dispatch: Kill.

Scythians: Inhabitants of the ancient country of Scythia, in the region of the Black Sea and Aral Sea.

Betoken: A sign of.

Rack: Wood frame on which a body is stretched for torture.

Pretext: Pretense.

Piety: Holiness.

Valor: Bravery.

Profusion: A great amount.

Superfluous: Beyond what is required.

Intercourse: Association.

Wretches: Unfortunate people.

*have left the serenity of their own sky to come and see ours—were at **Rouen**, at the time when the late King Charles the Ninth was there. The King talked to them for a long time; they were shown our ways, our **pomp**, the form of the fine city. After that someone asked their opinion, and wanted to know what they had found most amazing. They replied that there were three things, of which I have forgotten the third, and I am very sorry for it; but I still remember two of them. They said that in the first place they thought it very strange that so many grown men, bearded, strong, and armed, who were around the King (it is likely that they were talking about the Swiss of his guard) should submit to obey a child, and that one of them was not chosen to command instead; secondly (they have a way in their language of speaking of men as halves of one another), that they had noticed that there were among us men full and **gorged** with all sorts of good things, and that their other halves were beggars at their doors, emaciated with hunger and poverty; and they thought it strange that these needy halves could suffer such an injustice, and did not take the others by the throat, or set fire to their houses.*

*I had a long talk with one of them; but I had an interpreter who followed my meaning so badly, and who was so **hindered** by his stupidity in taking my ideas, that I could get hardly any satisfaction from the man. When I asked him what profit he gained from his superior position among his people (for he was captain, and our sailors called him king), he told me that it was to march foremost in war. How many men followed him? He pointed to a piece of ground, to signify as many as such a space could hold; it might have been four or five thousand men. Did all this authority expire with the war? He said that this much remained, that when he visited the villages dependent on him, they made paths for him through the underbrush by which he might pass quite comfortably.*

All this is not too bad. But wait! They don't wear trousers.

What happened next...

In the late sixteenth and seventeenth centuries *Essays* was regarded simply as a collection of wise sayings. Few people appreciated the fact that Montaigne had expressed his own

Rouen: A city in France.

Pomp: Meaningless public ceremony or display.

Gorged: Stuffed.

Hindered: Obstructed.

thoughts and feelings, and many found his intimate, personal approach to be irrelevant, even shocking. Religious writers such as Francis of Sales (1567–1622) and Blaise Pascal (1623–1662) criticized his skepticism as being anti-Christian and his emphasis on self as being immoral. Those who did admire his writings considered him the model of the well-educated nobleman who viewed the world with amused detachment from the privacy of his study. Attitudes toward *Essays* began to change in the eighteenth century, however. For instance, the French writer Jean-Jacques Rousseau (1712–1778) recognized Montaigne's contribution to the search for individual human identity through the free exploration of his own inner thoughts. By the twentieth century Montaigne's essays were being read by people throughout the world. He had a strong influence on modern writers, who valued his views on sorting out the contradictory experiences of being human in a complex age.

Did you know...

- In 1565 Montaigne married Françoise de la Chassaigne, daughter of a co-councilor in the Bordeaux Parlement. They had six daughters, of whom only one survived to adulthood. Montaigne and his wife were apparently compatible, but the marriage was sometimes cool—he believed that marriage ranked somewhat lower than friendship. In "Of Friendship" as quoted in *Selected Essays* translated by Donald M. Frame, Montaigne wrote:

    > As for marriage, besides its being a bargain to which only the entrance is free, its continuance being constrained and forced, depending otherwise than on our will, and a bargain ordinarily made for other ends, there supervene [interfere] a thousand foreign tangles to unravel, enough to break the thread and trouble the course of a lively affection; whereas in friendship there are no dealings or business except itself.

- The English-language edition of *Essays* by John Florio was a source for William Shakespeare's play *The Tempest* as well as the works of other playwrights.

For More Information

Books
Montaigne, Michel de. *Selected Essays*. Translated by Donald M. Frame. New York: Van Nostrand, 1941.

Web Sites

Brians, Paul. *Montaigne, Michel de, 'On Cannibals.'* [Online] Available http://www.wsu.edu:8080/~wldciv/world_civ_reader/world_civ_reader_2/montaigne.html, April 10, 2002.

"Gournay, Marie de." *Early Modern French Women Writers.* [Online] Available http://erc.lib.umn.edu/dynaweb/french/@Generic__CollectionView, April 10, 2002.

"Marie de Gournay, (1565–1645)." *Sunshine for Women.* [Online] Available http://www.pinn.net/~sunshine/march99/gournay2.html, April 10, 2002.

"Montaigne, Michel de." *Encyclopedia.com.* [Online] Available http://www.encyclopedia.com/searchpool.asp?target=@DOCTITLE%20Montaigne%20%20Michel%20Eyquem%20%20seigneur%20de, April 10, 2002.

"Montaigne, Michel de." *Essays.* Translated by Charles Cotton. [Online] Available http://www.orst.edu/instruct/phl302/texts/montaigne/m-essays_contents.html, April 10, 2002.

Margaret Cavendish

Excerpt from The Description of the New World
Called the Blazing World *(1666)*

**Reprinted in *The Description of the New World
Called the Blazing World and Other Writings***

Edited by Kate Lilley
Published in 1999

The English author and intellectual Margaret Cavendish (1623–1674), first duchess of Newcastle, wrote in the greatest variety of genres of any person of the late Renaissance period. The Renaissance was a cultural revolution that began in Italy in the mid-1300s. It was initiated by scholars called humanists who promoted the human-centered values of ancient Greece and Rome. Humanist ideals were soon influencing the arts, literature, philosophy, science, religion, and politics in Italy. During the early fifteenth century, innovations of the Italian Renaissance began spreading into the rest of Europe and reached a peak in the sixteenth century. Her works consisted of scientific philosophy, two volumes of plays, poetry, fantasies, essays, letters, a biography of her husband, and an autobiography. Not only did she take the daring step of becoming a published author—English women rarely wrote for a public audience at the time—but she also signed her own name to her books.

Cavendish is isolated but seeks fame

Cavendish was a complex figure. While she was a staunch loyalist (supporter of the monarchy), she had few ties

Margaret Cavendish

Margaret Cavendish was born in 1624 in Colchester, England. She was the youngest of eight children of Thomas Lucas, a wealthy landowner, and his wife. Thomas Lucas died in 1625. When the English Civil War (1642–48) broke out in 1642, rebel forces overthrew the monarchy of King Charles I (1600–1669; ruled 1625–49). The Lucas family then moved to the royalist, or pro-monarchy, town of Oxford south of London, where Margaret was appointed maid of honor at the court of Queen Henrietta Maria (1609–1669). Two years later Margaret accompanied the queen into exile (forced absence from one's country) in Paris, France. Around 1645, while in Paris, Margaret married William Cavendish (1592–1676), duke of Newcastle, a royalist military hero who was thirty years older than she.

King Charles I was beheaded in 1649 and the Commonwealth government was established in England. Newcastle was officially banished from the country and his property was seized. He and Margaret went to Antwerp, Belgium, where they lived in exile. In 1651 Margaret returned to England with her brother-in-law, Charles Cavendish, to seek repayment for William's estate. The request was denied. Remaining in England for nearly two years, Margaret wrote her first works, *Poems, and Fancies* and *Philosophical Fancies*, which were both issued in 1653. After returning to Antwerp in 1653 she wrote four more books, thus beginning a productive, twenty-year career. The Newcastles went back to England in 1660, when King Charles II (1630–1685; ruled 1660–85) took the throne at the beginning of the Restoration (reinstatement of the monarchy). They settled at William's estate, Welbeck in Nottinghamshire, where Margaret continued to write until her death in 1673.

with the Anglican Church (the official religion of England). Moreover, she often published essays and letters that criticized England's monarchy and rigid social class system. She wrote radical commentaries on women's social, political, intellectual, and legal standing. Despite her feminist ideals, Cavendish often painted women as weak, emotional creatures dependent upon the goodness and support of men. While others thought she was privileged, she frequently portrayed herself a social outcast. She felt she had been isolated from the intellectual mainstream of universities and scholarly activity because she was a woman. She found fulfillment when writing in the solitude of her study, but also sought public recognition. Cavendish associated with intellectuals and remained in-

formed about the latest cultural developments. For instance, she dined with the French philosopher René Descartes (1596–1650) and she visited the all-male Royal Society, the prestigious scientific organization in London. Nevertheless, critics would not overlook her lack of formal training, since she knew no foreign languages and had no classical or scholarly education. Cavendish met with constant ridicule because she wrote so many works on so many different subjects. Although she had a prolific career, Cavendish is best known today for *The Description of a New World Called the Blazing World* (1666).

The English author and intellectual Margaret Cavendish wrote in the greatest variety of genres of any person of the late Renaissance period. Her book *The Description of a New World Called the Blazing World* is considered the first science fiction novel.
©Bettmann/Corbis. Reproduced by permission of Corbis Corporation.

Things to Remember While Reading an Excerpt from *The Description of the New World Called the Blazing World:*

• *Blazing World* tells the story of a young lady who is abducted by a foreign merchant and taken by ship into another world, the Blazing World. After the merchant and the ships's crew freeze to death during the passage into the new world, they thaw out and spread corruption. The young lady is then transformed into an empress. Ruling over the Blazing World as a warrior queen, she puts down rebellions and commands armies of bird-men, worm-men, bear-men, and other warriors in a series of fantastic adventures.

• In this excerpt the Empress sends the bird-men and worm-men to burn the towns of princes who did not meet her demands. She commands them to use water, which she has made flammable, to destroy the towns. Her armies' efforts are aided first by a great tide (rising of the sea) and a torrential rain that flood the towns. After several weeks the Empress achieves victory and declares herself the ruler of the Blazing World. She stages a spectacular ceremony and entertainment at sea. The Empress then delivers a triumphant speech to the conquered princes, vowing to assist the monarch of her native land, King of ESFI, in a war against his enemies.

Excerpt from The Description of the New World Called the Blazing World

*But before both the bird- and worm-men began their journey, the Empress commanded the bear-men to view through their telescopes what towns and cities those were that would not submit; and having a full information thereof, she instructed the bird- and bear-men what towns they should begin withal; in the meanwhile she sent to all the princes and **sovereigns** of those nations, to let them know that she would give them proof of her power, and **check** their **obstinacies** by burning some of their smaller towns,... At last ... the worm-men laid some fire-stones under the foundation of every house, and the bird-men placed some at the tops of them, so that both by rain and by some other moisture within the earth, the stones could not fail of burning. The bird-men in the meantime having learned some few words of their [the princes' and sovereigns'] language, told them, that the next time it did rain, their towns would be all on fire; at which they were amazed to hear men speak in the air; but **withal** they laughed when they heard them say that rain should fire their towns, knowing that the effect of water was to quench, not produce fire.*

*At last a rain came, and upon a sudden all their houses appeared in a flaming fire, and the more water they poured on them, the more they did flame and burn; which struck such a fright and terror into all the neighbouring cities, nations and kingdoms, that for fear the like would happen to them, they and all the rest of the parts of the world granted the Empress's desire, and submitted to the monarch and sovereign of her native country, the King of ESFI; **save** one, which having seldom or never any rain, but only dews, which would soon be spent in a great fire, slighted her power: the Empress being desirous to make it stoop, as well as the rest, knew that every year it was watered by a flowing **tide**, which lasted some weeks; and although their houses stood high from the ground, yet they were built upon supporters which were fixed into the ground. Wherefore*

Sovereigns: Leaders.

Check: Stop.

Obstinacies: Refusals to obey.

Withal: Together.

Save: Except.

Tide: Rising of the sea.

she commanded both her bird- and worm-men to lay some of the fire-stones at the bottom of those supporters, and when the tide came in, all their houses were of fire, which did so **rarefy** the water, that the tide was soon turned into vapour, and this vapour again into air; which caused not only a destruction of their houses, but also a general **barrenness** over all their country that year, and forced them to submit as well as the rest of the world had done.

Thus the Empress did not only save her native country, but made it the absolute monarchy of all that world; and both the effects of her power and her beauty did kindle a great desire in all the greatest princes to see her; who hearing that she was resolved to return into her own Blazing World, they all **entreated** the favour, that they might wait on Her Majesty before she went. The Empress sent word, that she should be glad to grant their requests; but having no other place of reception for them, she desired that they should be pleased to come into the open seas with their ships, and make a circle of a pretty large **compass,** and then her own ships should meet them, and close up the circle, and she would present her self with the view of all those that came to see her: which answer was joyfully received by all the mentioned princes, who came, some sooner, and some later, each according to the distance of his country, and the length of the voyage. And being all met in the form and manner **aforesaid,** the Empress appeared upon the face of the water in her imperial robes; in some part of her hair she had placed some of the star-stone, near her face, which added such a lustre and glory to it, that it caused a great admiration in all that were present, who believed her to be some **celestial** creature, or rather an uncreated goddess, and they all had a desire to worship her; for surely, said they, no mortal creature can have such a splendid and **transcendent** beauty, nor can any have so great a power as she has, to walk upon the waters, and to destroy whatever she pleases, not only whole nations, but a whole world.

The Empress expressed to her own countrymen, who were also her interpreters to the rest of the princes that were present, that she would give them an entertainment at the darkest time of night; which being come, the fire-stones were lighted, which made both air and seas appear of a bright shining flame, insomuch that they put all spectators into an extreme fright, who verily believed, they should all be destroyed; which the Empress perceiving, caused all the lights of the fire-stones to be put out, and only showed herself in her garments of light: the bird-men carried her upon their backs into the air, and there she appeared as glorious as the sun. Then she was set

Rarefy: To make thin.

Barrenness: Bareness; lack of vegetation.

Entreated: Begged.

Compass: Surrounding area.

Aforesaid: Previously mentioned.

Celestial: Heavenly.

Transcendent: Surpassing ordinary.

*down upon the seas again, and presently there was heard the most melodious and sweetest **consort** of voices, as ever was heard out of the seas, which was made by the fish-men; this consort was answered by another, made by the bird-men in the air, so that it seemed as if sea and air had spoke and answered each other by way of singing **dialogues,** or after the manner of those plays that are acted by singing voices.*

But when it was upon break of day, the Empress ended her entertainment, and at full daylight all the princes perceived that she went into the ship wherein the prince and monarch of her native country was, the King of ESFI with whom she had several conferences; and having assured him of the readiness of her assistance whensoever he required it, telling him withal, that she wanted no intelligence, she went forth again upon the waters, and being in the midst of the circle made by those ships that were present, she desired them to draw somewhat nearer, that they might hear her speak; which being done, she declared her self in this following manner:

*Great, heroic, and famous monarchs: I came hither to assist the King of ESFI against his enemies, he being unjustly assaulted by many several nations, which would fain take away his hereditary rights and prerogatives of the narrow seas; at which unjustice Heaven was much displeased; and for the injuries he received from his enemies, rewarded him with an absolute power, so that now he is become the head-monarch of all this world; which power, though you may envy, yet you can no ways **hinder** him; for all those that endeavour to resist his power, shall only get loss for their labour, and no victory for their profit. Wherefore my advice to you all is, to pay him **tribute:** justly and truly, that you may live peaceably and happily, and be rewarded with the blessings of Heaven, which I wish you from my soul.*

After the Empress had thus finished her speech to the princes of the several nations of that world, she desired that their ships might fall back, which being done, her own fleet came into the circle, without any visible assistance of sails or tide; and herself being entered into her own ship, the whole fleet sunk immediately into the bottom of the seas, and left all the spectators in a deep amazement; neither would she suffer any of her ships to come above the waters until she arrived into the Blazing World.

Consort: Concert.

Dialogues: Conversations.

Hinder: Obstruct.

Tribute: Loyalty.

A frontispiece with an engraving of Margaret Cavendish. She produced a more substantial body of work than any other mid-seventeenth-century woman. *Reproduced by permission of Mary Evans Picture Library.*

What happened next...

Cavendish continued to write and prepare her books for publication until her sudden death in 1673, at age fifty. She produced a more substantial body of work than any other mid-seventeenth-century woman. Her writings received a mixed reception—more negative than positive. While she may have been only a minor literary figure in the late 1600s, during the twentieth century her works gained serious attention from literary scholars, historians of science, women's historians, and those who study women philosophers. More recently scholars have studied Cavendish as a writer of fantasy, autobiography, and biography.

Did you know...

- *Blazing World* is often called one of the first science fiction novels. Many twentieth-century scholars also regard the book as a daring exploration of women's power.

- Cavendish was nicknamed "Mad Madge" because people thought she was mentally unstable. She was ridiculed for her self-promotion, her willingness to debate famous male thinkers, and her strong feminist views. She also attracted negative attention by dressing unconventionally, often wearing a combination of women's and men's clothing.

For More Information

Books

Cavendish, Margaret. *The Description of a New World Called the Blazing World and Other Writings*. Edited by Kate Lilley. New York: Penguin Classics, 1994.

Web Sites

Norton Topics Online: Van Schuppen, Engraving [portrait] of Margaret Cavendish. [Online] Available http://www.wwnorton.com/nael/NTO/18thC/worlds/imcavendish.htm, April 10, 2002.

Protestant Reformation

Humanist concepts had a profound impact on religion, as scholars began translating and reexamining biblical texts. Humanists not only challenged church teachings based on questionable interpretations of the Bible but also they also challenged the power that church officials held over the European people. The Protestant Reformation, aided by the mass production of pamphlets criticizing the Catholic Church, swept across Europe in the sixteenth century. At the same time, the Catholic Church was publicizing its own system of reforms, known as the Catholic Reformation. It could be said that the Protestant Reformation and the Catholic Reformation were conducted in large part through published documents. Reformers released pamphlets calling for changes in church practices and teachings. Popes issued official orders implementing reforms and supporting church traditions. Leaders of both religions wrote inspirational texts, biblical studies, theological treatises, and position papers on controversial issues. Hundreds of these documents have survived into the twenty-first century, providing historians and general readers with a vivid account of the tumultuous Reformation era.

The Protestant Reformation was initiated in 1517 by Martin Luther, a German priest who was opposed to the Roman Catholic Church's practice of selling indulgences. He took action by posting a list of his grievances, titled "The Ninety-Five Theses or Disputation on the Power and Efficacy of Indulgences" (now known as "The Ninety-Five Theses"), on the door of the church at Wittenberg University. This document was to transform life in Europe within a few brief decades. When Luther posted his theses he simply intended to start a formal debate. The debate never took place, but this document was immediately translated from Latin into German and distributed via the printing press elsewhere in Europe. Luther's ideas were soon promoted by other reformers. Among them was the Swiss preacher Huldrych Zwingli, who followed Luther in criticizing indulgences and then went on to attack other Catholic Church abuses. Zwingli presented sixty-seven theses, now known as "The Sixty-Seven Articles of Ulrich Zwingli," in which he offered solutions to major problems in the church.

Even in the earliest stage of the Protestant Reformation there was disharmony among reformers. Zwingli quickly abandoned Lutheranism and promoted his own brand of Protestantism. The French-born Swiss reformer John Calvin, who became the most influential Protestant leader, also did not agree with many of Luther's ideas. From his base in Basel, Switzerland, Calvin advocated an even stricter form of Protestantism called Calvinism. He wrote many works on his theological theories. Among the most influential was *Ecclesiastical Ordinances,* which Calvin used as the basis of a reorganized local church government in Basel in the mid-1500s.

The teachings of Luther, Zwingli, and Calvin were adopted in many parts of Europe, but they did not necessarily reflect the views of everyone who claimed to be a Protestant. In fact, new Protestant sects were constantly forming and reforming. One of the earliest and strongest sects was the Swiss Brethren, called the Anabaptists, a splinter group organized by former followers of Zwingli. Anabaptists were seen as a threat by both Protestants and Catholics, and they were suppressed wherever they settled. So many Anabaptists were executed that by the end of the sixteenth century they soon came to be regarded as martyrs. Shortly before being executed, a Dutch Anabaptist woman named Elizabeth wrote a letter containing spiritual guidance to her infant daughter.

Martin Luther

Excerpt from "The Ninety-Five Theses or Disputation on the Power and Efficacy of Indulgences" (1517)

Reprinted in *Confessions and Catechisms of the Reformation*

Edited by Mark A. Noll
Published in 1997

The fifteenth and sixteenth centuries were a time of transition from the Middle Ages (c. 400 –1400; also called the medieval period) to the modern era. The medieval period had been an era of walls and of faith. Massive stone walls had been built round each little town to protect against the evils of the outside world. Inside these walls, medieval people knew their place. They were craftsmen, noblemen, churchmen, farmers, and knights (noblemen soldiers). They did not question their duties because they were safe and had faith in the way things were run. At that time the Roman Catholic Church (a Christian religion headed by a pope and based in Rome, Italy) controlled all aspects of social, political, and religious life. It was the largest institution in western Europe and consisted of an elaborate hierarchy (ranks of officials)—the pope, cardinals (officials ranking below the pope), bishops (heads of church districts), canons (legal administrators), priests (heads of local churches), and numerous other clergymen. The pope was considered infallible (always correct), and he was the most powerful ruler in Europe. The Catholic Church was also immensely wealthy, owning vast properties and collecting huge sums in taxes, tithes (one-tenth of church members' income), and other forms of payment from the people.

Beginning in the fifteenth century, the medieval view of the world underwent radical change in response to new discoveries. By the end of the fifteenth century, for instance, Portuguese explorers had rounded the Cape of Good Hope, and Christopher Columbus had reached the New World (the European term for the Americas). Renaissance humanists (scholars who revived the literary culture of ancient Greece and Rome) had freed scholarship and the arts from the sponsorship of the church. In so doing, humanists not only rediscovered the individual but also challenged the blind acceptance of authority and encouraged the individual search for truth through reason. Now people were seeking a better way to understand God in terms of their own experience.

Luther questions church

Into this changing world was born Martin Luther (1483–1546). Now known as the father of the Protestant Reformation, Luther was a German priest who single-handedly altered the course of European history. A native of Eisleben, Saxony (a state in Germany), Luther originally planned to become a lawyer. In 1501 he enrolled at the University of Erfurt, one of the oldest and most prestigious universities in Germany, and within four years he earned both bachelor's and master's degrees. In 1505 he had just begun the study of law and was on his way to a career in service to the church or to one of the many German princes (rulers of states). Then he abruptly abandoned the university for the disciplined life of a monastery (house for men in a religious order). This dramatic change occurred on July 2, 1505, while Luther was returning to the university from a visit with his parents. Along the way he was suddenly caught in a thunderstorm. As lightning struck nearby, he cried out in terror to his patron saint: "Save me, Saint Anne, and I will become a monk." Just two weeks later, Luther joined the Eremites of Saint Augustine, a religious order in Erfurt. He was ordained a priest within a year.

Luther was no ordinary monk, for he was deeply troubled by the teachings of the church. Since the early Middle Ages, Catholic leaders had taught that the church was the only link between the individual and God. The church provided salvation (deliverance from sin, or wrongdoing) to repentant sinners through the sacraments, or holy rituals, most notably communion (also called the Holy Eucharist). Administered in a ceremony called the mass, communion is a ritual in which bread and wine symbolize the body and blood of Jesus of Nazareth (called the Christ), the founder of Christianity. Also, the church taught that the individual had a duty to use his or her own free will (ability to make independent choices) to love and serve God. This was the way to earn salvation from God. In short, the individual participated in his or her own salvation through good works, or acts. Such teachings brought comfort to many, but they caused distress for Luther. His problem was that no matter how hard he "worked" at earning his salvation, he could not find any peace with God.

Luther found the answer to his spiritual problem sometime during the fall of 1515. By then he was a professor of theology (study of religion) at the University of Wittenberg and the overseer of eleven monasteries. The answer came while he was preparing a series of lectures in his study in monastery's tower. He was pondering the meaning of verse 17 in chapter 1 of the book of Romans in the New Testament (second part of the Bible, the Christian holy book): "For it is the righteousness of God revealed from faith to faith; as it is written, The just shall live by faith." In that little verse was contained the heart of Luther's problem, as well as the solution. He was perplexed by the two phrases, "the righteousness of God" and "The just shall live by faith." In accordance with church teachings, Luther understood "the righteousness of God" to mean that a righteous, even angry, God punishes all sinners. Such a view caused him to hate the God he knew he should love. Then, as Luther meditated over the verse, its meaning broke through: "I began to understand," he wrote later, "that the righteousness of God is that gift of God by which a righteous [morally upright] man lives, namely, faith, and that ... the merciful God justifies us by faith, as it is written: 'The righteous shall live by faith.'"

Reaches revolutionary conclusion

Luther had come to a revolutionary conclusion—that salvation comes through faith alone. He then reached

Indulgences

Indulgences began as gifts of money given to the clergy in appreciation or gratitude for forgiveness of sins, or wrongdoings. Soon, however, indulgences began to represent an outward showing of grief for sins. People would pay for indulgences to prove to the church and others that they were truly repentant for their sins. In the thirteenth century, the Catholic Church formulated what was called the "treasury of merits." It was a spiritual bank of sorts that "contained" the good works performed by Jesus Christ, the saints, and all pious Christians. In other words, because

Jesus and the saints had lived better lives than necessary to get into heaven, their good deeds had been left on Earth in the treasury of merits. Good deeds from this treasury could be redistributed to Christian believers in the form of indulgences. One would give money to his or her clergyman, who would in turn make a "withdrawal" from the spiritual bank. This system was supposed to reduce the punishments one suffered in purgatory, but many did not understand it. It was widely believed that people could sin as much as possible and still buy their way into heaven.

an even more startling conclusion: This truth is revealed in the Bible, not through the mass and other sacraments administered by priests. Therefore, all of the clergy, from the pope down to the parish priest, were unnecessary. Luther did not immediately challenge the church with this hypothesis. What spurred him to action was the appearance, in 1517, of a monk peddling indulgences, payments to church officials for forgiveness of sins, (see accompanying box) outside Wittenberg. The monk was selling indulgences on behalf of the new Archbishop of Mainz, twenty-three-year-old Albert von Hohenzollern, who had "purchased" his position. To pay back the funds he borrowed from the Fugger bank in Augsburg to finance the purchase, Albert was authorized by Pope Leo X (1475–1521; reigned 1513–21) to sell indulgences in Germany.

The abuse of the indulgence system was evident in the aggressive sales tactics of John Tetzel (1465–1519), an experienced indulgence salesman who appeared outside Luther's door in October 1517. Tetzel was selling indulgences to finance the new Saint Peter's Basilica, which was under

Pope Nicholas V granting indulgences to a king and queen. Martin Luther felt impelled to respond to the obvious misuse of indulgences. *©Bettmann/ Corbis. Reproduced by permission of Corbis Corporation.*

construction in Rome. He claimed that indulgences could be purchased for relatives already dead, or for sins one might commit in the future. "As soon as the coin in the coffer rings," Tetzel said, "the soul from purgatory springs."

Luther felt impelled to respond to the obvious misuse of indulgences. According to popular legend, on October 31, 1517 (the eve of All Saints' Day; now called Halloween), Luther defiantly nailed a document titled "Ninety-Five Theses or Disputation on the Power and Efficacy of Indulgences" to the door of the church at the University of Wittenberg. Some scholars downplay the drama of this act, suggesting that Luther simply tacked the "Ninety-Five Theses" to the church door, which served as a kind of bulletin board at the university. Others say he attached the theses to the letter he wrote to the Archbishop of Mainz, protesting the sale of indulgences. In any case, he intended the document as an invitation to his colleagues to debate the issue.

Things to Remember While Reading an Excerpt from "The Ninety-Five Theses or Disputation on the Power and Efficacy of Indulgences":

- In the "Ninety-Five Theses" Luther challenged indulgence sales and reprimanded the church for its financial exploitation of Germany. For instance, in Thesis 86 he inquired, "Why does not the pope, whose wealth is today greater than the wealth of the richest Crassus build this one basilica of Saint Peter with his own money rather than with the money of poor believers?" (Marcelus Licinius Crassus [c.115–53 B.C.E.] was a Roman financier and politician who accumulated a vast fortune.)

- Theses 1 through 25 trace Luther's main arguments against the practice of selling indulgences. He asserted that salvation should be based wholly on faith, which is derived from the Scripture, or text of the Bible, and cannot be granted by the pope or members of the clergy.

Martin Luther fastening his Ninety-Five Theses to a door at the church at Wittenberg. Although the Theses were only intended to result in intellectual debate, they ended up sparking the Protestant Reformation.

Reproduced by permission of The Granger Collection.

- In Theses 26 through 51 Luther outlined the proper spiritual obligations of the pope toward Christians. In Theses 52 through 95 he provided additional evidence of how the pope's misuse of indulgences violated the true spirit of Christianity.

- The following excerpt from "The Ninety-Five Theses" consists of Theses 1 through 25.

Excerpt from
"The Ninety-Five Theses or Disputation on the Power and Efficacy of Indulgences"

Out of love and zeal for truth and the desire to bring it to light, the following theses will be publicly discussed at Wittenberg under the chairmanship of the reverend father Martin Luther, master of arts and sacred theology and regularly appointed lecturer on these subjects at that place. He requests that those who cannot be present to debate orally with us will do so by letter.

In the name of our Lord Jesus Christ. Amen.

1. When our Lord and Master Jesus Christ said, "Repent" [Matt. 4:17], he willed the entire life of believers to be one of repentance.

*2. This word cannot be understood as referring to the **sacrament** of penance, that is, confession and satisfaction, as administered by the clergy.*

*3. Yet it does not mean solely inner repentance; such inner repentance is worthless unless it produces various outward **mortifications** of the flesh.*

*4. The penalty of sin remains as long as the hatred of self, that is, true inner repentance, until our entrance into the kingdom of **heaven**.*

*5. The pope neither desires nor is able to remit any penalties except those imposed by his own authority or that of the **canons**.*

*6. The pope cannot **remit** any guilt, except by declaring and showing that it has been remitted by God; or, to be sure, by remitting guilt in cases reserved to his judgement. If his right to grant re-*

Sacrament: Holy rite.

Mortifications: Self-inflicted pain or discomfort.

Heaven: Dwelling place of God and the blessed dead.

Canons: Rules or regulations made by a church council.

Remit: Lay aside partly or wholly.

mission in these cases were disregarded, the guilt would certainly remain unforgiven.

*7. God remits guilt to no one unless at the same time he humbles him in all things and makes him **submissive** to his vicar, the priest.*

8. The penitential canons are imposed only on the living, and, according to the canons themselves, nothing should be imposed on the dying.

*9. Therefore the **Holy Spirit** through the pope is kind to us insofar as the pope in his decrees always makes exception of the article of death and of necessity.*

*10. Those priests act ignorantly and wickedly who, in the case of the dying, reserve canonical penalties for **purgatory.***

*11. Those **tares** of changing the canonical penalty to the penalty of purgatory were evidently sown while the bishops slept [Matt. 13:25].*

*12. In former times canonical penalties were imposed, not after, but before **absolution,** as tests of true **contrition.***

13. The dying are freed by death from all penalties, are already dead as far as the canon laws are concerned, and have a right to be released from them.

*14. Imperfect **piety** or love on the part of the dying person necessarily brings with it great fear; and the smaller the love, the greater the fear.*

15. This fear or horror is sufficient in itself, to say nothing of other things, to constitute the penalty of purgatory, since it is very near the horror of despair.

*16. **Hell,** purgatory, and heaven seem to differ the same as despair, fear, and assurance of salvation.*

17. It seems as though for the souls in purgatory fear should necessarily decrease and love increase.

18. Furthermore, it does not seem proved, either by reason or Scripture, that souls in purgatory are outside the state of merit, that is, unable to grow in love.

19. Nor does it seem proved that souls in purgatory, at least not all of them, are certain and assured of their own salvation, even if we ourselves may be entirely certain of it.

Submissive: Submitting to others.

Holy Spirit: Third person of the Christian Trinity (God the Father, the Son, and the Holy Spirit).

Purgatory: The place between heaven and hell.

Tares: Seeds.

Absolution: Forgiveness of sins pronounced by a priest.

Contrition: The state of being truly penitent or sorry.

Piety: Dutifulness in religion.

Hell: Realm of the devil where the damned endure everlasting punishment.

20. Therefore the pope, when he uses the words "**plenary** remission of all penalties," does not actually mean "all penalties," but only those imposed by himself.

21. Thus those indulgence preachers are in error who say that a man is **absolved** from every penalty and saved by **papal** indulgences.

22. As a matter of fact, the pope remits to souls in purgatory no penalty which, according to canon law, they should have paid in this life.

23. If remission of all penalties whatsoever could be granted to anyone at all, certainly it would be granted only to the most perfect, that is, to very few.

24. For this reason most people are necessarily deceived by that indiscriminate and high-sounding promise of release from penalty.

25. That power which the pope has in general over purgatory corresponds to the power which any bishop or **curate** has in a particular way in his own **diocese** or parish.

What happened next...

Although Luther had directly challenged the pope's authority, Leo X did not move immediately to silence him. In 1519 Luther attended a debate at the University of Leipzig. The debate raged on for eighteen days before it was called off. Luther had defended his beliefs by stating that people should live their lives by following the Bible, not the pope. He said people could find their own salvation through faith—they did not need the church. Luther began writing his views in pamphlets, and his ideas soon spread throughout Germany. Many people backed him. In June 1520, Leo X issued a bull, or papal order, criticizing Luther and excommunicating (expelling) him from the church. When Luther received this document, he publicly burned it. The following April, Luther was summoned to the town of Worms, where an assembly of German princes (called the Diet) had been convened by the new Holy Roman Emperor, nineteen-year-old Charles V (1500–1558; ruled 1519–56). The Diet wanted Luther to withdraw his views. He refused, so Charles declared him an out-

Plenary: Complete in every respect.

Absolved: Set free from sin.

Papal: Relating to a pope or Roman Catholic Church.

Curate: Clergyman in charge of a parish.

Diocese: Territorial district of a bishop.

law of the church and ordered his arrest. But Frederick the Wise (1463–1525), Luther's friend and the prince who ruled Wittenberg, kidnapped Luther and hid him in Wartburg Castle, one of Frederick's residences near Eisenach. There, over the next eleven months, Luther spent his time translating the New Testament of the Bible from Latin into German.

Returning to Wittenberg in March 1522, Luther tried to unify his followers. By then, almost half the people of Ger-

Martin Luther before the Diet of Worms. Luther was called before the assembly to recant his views regarding the Catholic Church. *Reproduced by permission of Hulton Archive.*

many had adopted his views. Many called themselves "Lutherans" (only later did the reformers come to be known as Protestants). Yet the movement began to fragment almost immediately. The Bible may be the final authority, but according to Luther every believer is his own priest, his own interpreter of what the Bible says. Hence, numerous Protestant sects, or groups, were formed—and they are still being formed even today.

All that happened after the Diet of Worms was anticlimactic. Luther tried to halt the radicalism, or extreme views, of some of his followers. But fragmentation, not unity, was to characterize the future of the Protestant churches. In 1530 Philip Melanchthon (1497–1560), Luther's closest associate, drafted a confession, or statement, of faith. Both he and Luther hoped it might provide a basis for unity between the Lutherans and the Roman Catholic Church. Rejected by the Diet of Augsburg, Melanchthon's confession, called the "Augsburg Confession," became the basis for the doctrine (beliefs and teachings) of Lutheran churches. Luther introduced numerous reforms in the worship service. He placed an emphasis on preaching and teaching from the Bible, and he reintroduced music and congregational singing. A fine musician, Luther wrote many popular hymns, including *A Mighty Fortress Is Our God* and *Away in a Manger.* Throughout the remaining years of his life, Luther continued writing, preaching, and teaching. He died on February 18, 1546, four days after he had preached in Eisleben, his hometown. He was buried on the grounds of the church in Wittenberg.

Did you know...

- Most modern scholars agree that Luther never intended to begin a widespread reform movement within the Catholic Church. He merely wanted to spark academic debate about a serious issue. Initially, his protest fell on deaf ears, since the archbishop of Mainz was sharing the profits of indulgence sales with the pope. Had someone not translated the "Ninety-Five Theses" from Latin (the language used in all formal communications) into German, they might have gone unnoticed. With the aid of the recently invented printing press, the translation appeared throughout Germany. The theses were thus made available to theologians, scholars, and anyone else who could read German.

- In 1525, Luther married Katherine von Bora, a former nun (a woman who belongs to a religious order). They had six children, some of whom died early, and adopted eleven others. By all accounts, their home was a happy one. Luther called his wife "my beloved Katie," and she was a great source of strength for him.

- Saint Peter's Basilica was completed in 1614. The construction had been beset by design changes and construction delays since Pope Julius II originally ordered the rebuilding of the old Saint Peter's church in 1506. Altogether, six architects were involved in the project. Saint Peter's Basilica is now considered the crowning achievement of Renaissance architecture.

For More Information

Books

Fearon, Mike. *Martin Luther*. Minneapolis: Bethany House Publishers, 1986.

Noll, Mark A. *Confessions and Catechisms of the Reformation*. Vancouver, B.C.: Regent College Publishing, 1997.

Scheib, Asta. *Children of Disobedience: The Love Story of Martin Luther and Katharina von Bora: A Novel*. Translated by David Ward. New York: Crossroad, 2000.

Stepanek, Sally. *Martin Luther*. New York: Chelsea House, 1986.

Video Recordings

Martin Luther. Worcester, Pa.: Vision Video, 1990.

Web Sites

Halsall, Paul. "Martin Luther; Letter to the Archbishop of Mainz, 1517." *Medieval Sourcebook*. [Online] Available http://www.fordham.edu/halsall/source/lutherltr-indulgences.html, April 10, 2002.

"Luther, Martin." *MSN Encarta*. [Online] Available http://encarta.msn.com/find/concise.asp?z=1&pg=2&ti=04875000, April 10, 2002.

Martin Luther and the Reformation. [Online] Available http://mars.acnet.wnec.edu/~grempel/courses/wc2/lectures/luther.html, April 10, 2002.

Huldrych Zwingli

"The Sixty-Seven Articles of Ulrich Zwingli" (1523)
Reprinted in *Confessions and Catechisms of the Reformation*
Edited by Mark A. Noll
Published in 1977

While Martin Luther was taking his stand against the Roman Catholic Church in Germany (see **Martin Luther** entry), Swiss pastor Huldrych (also spelled Ulrich) Zwingli (1484–1531) was leading a similar movement in Zurich, Switzerland. In 1518 Zwingli followed Luther in denouncing the church's practice of selling indulgences (partial forgiveness of sins), then he went on to attack other abuses. Zwingli was a preacher at the Great Minster, the main church in Zurich, in 1519 when he began a series of lectures on the book of Matthew in the New Testament (second part of the Bible, the Christian holy book). In his lectures he used simple terms and referred to events in every day life. This approach contradicted the policies of the church. Catholic priests were considered authorities on the Bible and they were not allowed to help their parishioners interpret the Scripture. Despite some opposition from traditional priests, Zwingli's unusual method was soon adopted by his fellow priests at Great Minster.

On March 5, 1522, in the home of the printer Christoph Froschauer (died 1564), some of Zwingli's friends and supporters broke the rule of fasting (abstaining from food) during Lent by eating sausages. Lent is a forty-day period prior to Easter, the celebration of Christ's rising from the dead. (Christ is the name given to Jesus of Nazareth, founder of the Christian religion.) Christians devote this time to prayer, penance (showing sorrow for sins), and reflection. As a sign of fasting and additional penance, Catholics are not permitted to eat meat during Lent. Zwingli turned this event into a public issue in his sermon, which he followed with a pamphlet. Not only did he support the actions of Froschauer and the others, but he also claimed that it was the right of every individual to choose freely what to eat.

The question of fasting triggered discussion of other issues. In January 1523, Zwingli invited the leading clergy of various cantons (Swiss states), including the bishop of Constance (head of the church district based in Constance), to the Zurich town hall for a disputation. (In the sixteenth century a disputation was the generally accepted means for settling conflict.) Most of his opponents refused to accept the invitation, and the bishop sent his personal adviser as an observer. Zwingli presented sixty-seven theses (subjects for debate), which are now known as "The Sixty-Seven Articles of Ulrich Zwingli." In this document he offered solutions to major problems in the church. Since the audience consisted mainly of his supporters, he easily convinced them to accept his plan. Zwingli's sixty-seven theses therefore became an outline for religious reform in Zurich.

The following excerpts from "The Sixty-Seven Articles of Ulrich Zwingli" reflect the main issues raised by Zwingli.

While Martin Luther was taking his stand against the Roman Catholic Church in Germany, Huldrych Zwingli was leading a similar movement in Zurich, Switzerland.

Things to Remember While Reading Excerpts from "The Sixty-Seven Articles of Ulrich Zwingli":

- In his sixty-seven articles Zwingli defined numerous church abuses. Among practices no longer considered acceptable by him and his followers were pilgrimages (religious journeys), processions (ceremonies in which clergy file into a church), incense (material burned to produce a fragrant odor), noisy hymns, and the purchase of prayers and indulgences. Zwingli also advised his audience not to spend their money on such things as gambling and lavish clothing, but instead to use it to feed the poor and support widows and orphans.

- Zwingli took a stand against praying to saints (people declared as holy by the Catholic Church) and asking them for help and favors. He thought people could learn such qualities as humility, faith, and hope from the lives of the saints, but he believed in praying directly to God. Zwingli further questioned the belief that saints worked miracles. When he was a preacher at a monastery (house of a men's religious order) earlier in his career he had seen crowds of pilgrims flocking to shrines and praying for miracles, and he felt that the church was taking advantage of their superstition to get rich.

- Compare "The Sixty-Seven Articles of Ulrich Zwingli" with the "Ninety-Five Theses" of Martin Luther. Notice that both Zwingli and Luther rejected the teaching that the church is the sole intermediary, or link, between God and Christians. Each man believed that an individual's faith should be based solely on his or her understanding of the Scriptures, and that forgiveness of sins comes directly from God without the involvement of priests. Yet Luther was primarily attacking the sale of indulgences, whereas Zwingli challenged nearly every church practice and policy. Although Luther is called the father of the Protestant Reformation, Zwingli played a more active role in the early stage of the reform movement.

Excerpt from
"The Sixty-Seven Articles of Ulrich Zwingli"

I, Ulrich Zwingli, confess that I have preached in the worthy city of Zurich these sixty-seven articles or opinions on the basis of Scripture, which is called theopneustos *(that is, inspired by God). I offer* *to defend and **vindicate** these articles with Scripture. But if I have not understood Scripture correctly, I am ready to be corrected, but only from the same Scripture.*

Notice, Pope, What Follows!

*17. That Christ is the only, everlasting High Priest can be determined by the fact that those who have passed themselves off as high priests oppose, and even **repudiate,** the honor and power of Christ.*

How the Prosperity of the Clergy Should Be Christ

*23. Christ condemns the prosperity and splendor of the world. Therefore, we conclude that those who accumulate wealth for themselves in his name **slander** him monstrously when they make him **pretense** for their own greed and **wantonness.***

Prohibition of Foods

*24. Christians are not obligated to do works that God has not commanded. They may eat all foods at all times. From this we learn that **decretals** regulating cheese and bread are a Roman fraud.*

Of Festivals and Pilgrimages

25. Time and place have been made subject to Christ, not the Christian to them. From this is to be learned that those who bind Christians to times and places rob them of their proper freedom.

Cowls, Badges, and the Like

*26. Nothing is more displeasing to God than **hypocrisy**. From this we conclude that everything which makes itself out to be splendid before men is a great hypocrisy and **infamy**. So much for monks' **cowls**, badges, **tonsures,** and the like.*

Orders and Sects

*27. All Christians are brothers of Christ one with another and should call no one on earth father. So much for orders, **sects, cliques,** and the like.*

The Marriage of Clergy

28. Everything that God permits or has not forbidden is proper. From this we learn that marriage is proper for all people.

The Impure Priest Should Take a Wife

29. All those who are in the church sin if they do not make themselves secure through marriage once they understand that God has granted marriage to them for the sake of purity.

Vindicate: To free from blame.

Repudiate: To refuse to have anything to do with.

Slander: False charges that damage another's reputation.

Pretense: A false reason or excuse.

Wantonness: Lavishness.

Decretals: Decrees.

Hypocrisy: The act of expressing feelings or beliefs that one does not actually hold true.

Infamy: Disgrace.

Cowls: Long hooded cloaks worn by monks (men who belong to religious orders).

Tonsures: The shaving of a monks' head when admitted to the Roman Catholic Church.

Sects: Religious groups.

Cliques: Exclusive groups of people.

Vows of Purity

*30. Those who take a vow of **chastity** assume madly or child-ishly too much. From this is to be learned that those who make such vows are treating godly people wantonly.*

Of Excommunication

*31. No private person may **excommunicate** anyone else, but the church—that is, the communion of those among whom the one subject to excommunication lives—along with its guardians may act as a bishop.*

32. The only one who should be excommunicated is a person who commits a public scandal.

Of Unclaimed Goods

*33. Unclaimed goods should not be given to temples, **cloisters**, monks, priests, or **nuns,** but to the needy, if it is impossible to return them to their rightful owner.*

Secular Authority from God

*35. But **secular** authority does have rightful power and is sup-ported from the teaching and action of Christ.*

36. Everything that the so-called spiritual estate claims by right or for the protection of its rights belongs properly to the secular au-thorities, if they have a mind to be Christians.

37. To these authorities all Christians are obliged to be obedi-ent, with no exceptions;

38. So long as the authorities do not command anything in op-position to God.

39. Therefore all secular laws should be conformed to the divine will, which is to say, that they should protect the oppressed, even if the oppressed make no complaint.

*40. Only these secular authorities have the power to put someone to death without provoking God. But only those should be executed who **perpetrated** a public scandal, unless God has decreed otherwise.*

*41. If secular rulers properly serve with counsel and assistance the ones for whom God has given them responsibility, they in turn are obligated to offer them bodily **sustenance.***

42. But if rulers act unfaithfully and not according to the guid-ing principles of Christ, they may be replaced by God.

Chastity: Abstention from sex.

Excommunicate: To deprive a person of the right of church membership.

Cloisters: Monasteries or nunneries.

Nuns: Women belonging to a religious order.

Secular: Not belonging to a religious order or congregation.

Perpetrated: Committed as in a crime.

Sustenance: Supplying the necessities of life.

43. *The sum of the matter is that the best and most secure government exists where the ruler governs with God alone, but the most evil and insecure where the ruler governs according to his own heart.*

Of Prayer

44. *True worshipers call upon God in spirit and in truth, without a lot of fuss before men.*

45. ***Hypocrites*** *do their deeds to be seen before men; they receive their reward in this age.*

46. *It must therefore follow that singing or* ***clamoring*** *in church, carried on without devotion and only for the praise of self, is done either for renown from men or profit.*

Of Offense

47. *A person should choose to suffer physical death before offending a Christian or bringing a Christian into disgrace.*

48. *The one who takes offense out of* ***imbecility*** *or ignorance, without cause, should not be allowed to remain sick or mean-spirited; rather, such a one should be nurtured to recognize what is really sin and what is not.*

49. *I know of no greater offense than that priests are not allowed to have lawful wives, while they are allowed to pay* ***concubines.*** *What a disgrace!*

Of Forgiveness of Sins

50. *God alone forgives sins, only through Christ Jesus his Son, our Lord.*

51. *Whoever* ***ascribes*** *this power to the creature takes away God's glory and gives it to someone who is not God. This is truly* ***idolatry.***

52. *Therefore, confession to a priest or a neighbor should not be done for the forgiveness of sins, but for the sake of receiving counsel.*

53. *Assigned works of satisfaction (except excommunication) are the product of human counsel; they do not take away sin; and they are imposed on others in order to terrorize them.*

Of Purgatory

57. *The true holy Scripture knows nothing of a* ***purgatory*** *after this life.*

58. *The judgement of the departed is known to God alone.*

Hypocrites: Those who put on a false appearance of religion or virtue.

Clamoring: Noisy shouting.

Imbecility: State of being feebleminded.

Concubines: Women whom men live with but to whom they are not married.

Ascribes: Refers to a supposed source.

Idolatry: Worship of a physical object, such as a statue or picture, as a god.

Purgatory: The place between heaven and hell.

59. And the less God has caused to make known to us about it, the less we should try to find out about it.

*60. I do not condemn it if a person concerned about the dead calls upon God to show them mercy. Yet to fix the time for this (seven years for a **mortal sin**) and to lie about such matters for the sake of gain is not human but **diabolical.***

Of the Priesthood and Its Ordained

*61. Of the kind of **ordination** that priests in recent times have invented, the holy Scripture knows nothing.*

62. Scripture recognizes no priests except those who proclaim God's Word.

63. Scripture asks that honor be offered to those who preach the Word, that is, that they be given physical sustenance.

Of Dealing with Misdeeds

64. Those who acknowledge their misdeeds should not be required to suffer for anything else, but should be allowed to die in peace. Thereafter any goods they leave to the church should be administered in a Christian way.

65. God will certainly deal with those who refuse to acknowledge their misdeeds. Therefore, we should not do them any bodily harm, unless they are leading others astray so obviously that it cannot be ignored.

*But let no one undertake to argue with **sophistry** or human wisdom, but let Scripture be the judge (Scripture breathes the Spirit of God), so that you can either find the truth or, if you have found it, hold on to it.*

Amen. God grant it!

What happened next...

During the years to come, Zwingli turned Zurich into an evangelical city. ("Evangelical" was a term used to refer to the reform movement in Germany.) Those who disagreed with Zwingli were forced either to comply or to leave. As

Mortal sin: A deliberately committed sin that deprives the soul of sanctifying grace.

Diabolical: Characteristic of the devil (figure of evil).

Ordination: The act of being invested officially with a ministerial or priestly authority.

Sophistry: Subtly deceptive reasoning or argumentation.

early as 1524, some of Zwingli's supporters claimed his reforms did not go far enough. Among them were the Anabaptists, who formed their own movement called the Swiss Brethren (see **Elizabeth** entry). They were seen as a threat by the Zwinglians, who banished Anabaptists from Zurich. In 1526 a Catholic-dominated conference was held in Baden, Switzerland. Zwingli was invited but he did not attend because he feared for his personal safety. The council condemned his reforms as the works of the "Antichrist [enemy of Christ] of the Great Minster."

On January 6, 1528, a disputation was allowed to take place in Bern, Switzerland. The debate lasted until the end of January, leaving no doubt that reforms Zwingli had demanded in Zurich would be carried out in the canton of Bern. One region, the Bernr Oberland, tried to resist, asking the neighboring states of Valais, Uri, and Unterwalden for spiritual and, eventually, military support. To reprimand the rebellious subjects, Bern sent in troops. The Bernr Oberland protestors soon

A scene from a conference in Marburg, Germany, between the various leaders of the Reformation movement. The conference was an attempt to reconcile the growing theological differences especially between Martin Luther and Huldrych Zwingli (standing center right). *Reproduced by permission of Hulton Archive.*

gave up and accepted reforms. Zwingli had reached the summit of his power and influence. He had long dreamed of forming a Protestant Swiss Confederation (an alliance of cantons in Switzerland), but he needed the help of allies in Germany.

Zwingli dies in battle

Zwingli finally met Luther the first time at a conference in Marburg, Germany, in 1529. The participants drew up fifteen articles that defined the Protestant faith. The Marburg meeting took place between the two Kappel Wars, religious conflicts between Catholics and Protestants. A truce was signed by both parties in 1529, but neither side seemed completely satisfied. When Zwingli returned home from the meeting, events seemed to develop in his favor. But shortly thereafter he met open resistance from the Catholic cantons, which were joined by opponents in his own ranks. Zwingli proposed a quick military campaign to put down opposition. Soon news reached Zurich that Catholic forces had gathered near Zug. Zurich's troops hurried in from all sides, but it was impossible to form orderly units on such short notice. Facing the well-prepared Catholic troops near Kappel in October 1531, the Protestant army of about fifteen hundred men fought bravely, but with no chance of victory. After only a few days, the Protestant alliance was defeated. Zurich lost about five hundred men in battle, among them its spiritual leader, Huldrych Zwingli. After Zwingli's death, his colleague Heinrich Bullinger (1504–1575) became the pastor at Great Minster and the leader of the reform movement in Switzerland. In 1536 Bullinger played an important role in compiling the First Helvetic Confession, a statement of reform goals based largely on Zwingli's views. In 1549 Bullinger joined the French reformer **John Calvin** (1509–1564; see entry) in drafting the Consensus of Tigurnius, which moved Swiss reform efforts toward Calvinism (a strict form of Protestantism).

Did you know...

- Many Catholic clergymen in northern Switzerland were married, and Zwingli was among them. Secretly, he had married Anna Reinhart and had fathered several children. Together with ten other priests he sent a petition to the bishop of Constance asking for church recognition of their marriages. To strengthen their argument, they pointed out that the "bishops" (founders) of the early Church had been married men.

- Zwingli contended that pictures and statues of saints only encouraged idolatry, so they should be taken down. Many of his most enthusiastic followers took his word literally, and from 1523 until 1525 they stripped decorations, statues, and pictures from all Catholic churches in Zurich. They frequently used violent tactics, causing disturbances in cantons that refused to adopt Zwingli's new methods.

- The reform council in Zurich brought formal charges against Anabaptists and executed some of them. In 1527 the Anabaptist leader Felix Mantz was one of those put to death. Zwingli supported this harsh policy, and it contributed to a decline in his popularity.

- Luther was said to have had a haughty way about him when speaking to Zwingli. Luther considered Zwingli a coarse fanatic (one who holds extreme beliefs) who was trying to show off his Greek and Latin because his German was so poor. When the two men finally met at the conference in Marburg in 1529, they reportedly parted without shaking hands.

For More Information

Book

Gäbler, Ulrich. *Huldrych Zwingli: His Life and Work*. Translated by Ruth C. L. Gritsch. Philadelphia: Fortress Press, 1986.

Web Sites

Protestant Reformation. [Online] Available http://www.mun.ca/rels/hrollmann/reform/reform.html, April 10, 2002.

"Zwingli, Ulrich." *Encyclopedia.com.* [Online] Available http://www.encyclopedia.com/searchpool.asp?target=@DOCTITLE%20Zwingli%20%20Huldreich%20or%20Ulrich, April 10, 2002.

Zwingli and Luther. [Online] Available http://www.bible.org/docs/history/schaff/vol7/schaf176.htm, April 10, 2002.

John Calvin

Excerpt from Ecclesiastical Ordinances
Edited by Hans J. Hillerbrand
Published in 1968

John Calvin (1509–1564) was perhaps the most influential leader of the Protestant Reformation, a movement to reform the Roman Catholic Church in Europe. He was involved in reform efforts at the same time as **Martin Luther** (see entry), the German theology professor who initiated the Reformation. Calvin interpreted Christianity more strictly than Luther, however, establishing his own distinct form of Protestantism in Geneva, Switzerland. Under his tireless direction, Geneva became the focus of successful and far-reaching evangelism (personal commitment to the teachings of Jesus Christ, founder of Christianity), which was the foundation of many present-day Protestant churches.

Calvin brings evangelism to Geneva

John Calvin was born Jean Cauvin in Noyon, France, in 1509. His father, Gérard Cauvin, was a lawyer who worked for the local bishop. His mother, Jeanne Lefranc, was the daughter of a fairly well-to-do innkeeper. Calvin was educated in Noyon until 1523, when he was awarded a benefice, or church office in which income is used for education. He enrolled at the University of Paris, where he received an extensive humanist education. (Humanism was the study of ancient Greek and Latin works and early biblical texts.) Calvin remained at Paris for five years with the intention of entering the Catholic priesthood, but in 1528 his father ordered him to switch from theology (study of religion) to law. At some point he converted to Protestantism. Late in 1533 there was a general crackdown on Protestants by the royal government, causing Calvin to flee Paris.

Calvin left France in 1534. Traveling under the assumed name Martianus Lucianius, he settled in Basel, Switzerland. He spent the next two years in private study. In 1536 he published the first edition of his major work, *Christianae religionis institutio* (Institutes of the Christian Religion; see accompanying box). One evening in June 1536, Calvin stopped in Geneva to spend the night. He intended to continue on his journey the following day, but the local evangelical preacher, Guillaume Farel (1489–1565), had another idea. Farel convinced Calvin that it was his duty to God to remain where he was most needed. Farel had hoped to expel Catholicism from the city, which had recently won its independence from the church. Calvin agreed to stay in Geneva, and with Farel he worked to establish Protestantism within the city. Within a couple of years, however, both men were banished for being too strict and for encouraging French Huguenots (Protestants from France) to move to Geneva. Calvin then went to Strasbourg, where he taught at an academy, preached, and developed his ideas on the nature of the ideal Christian church. Calvin's friends in Strasbourg urged him to find a wife. In 1540 he married Idelette Bure, the widow of one of his converts, who already had a son and a daughter. The couple's only child died shortly after birth in 1542. Idelette died seven years later, but Calvin never remarried.

John Calvin was perhaps the most influential leader of the Protestant Reformation. *Photograph courtesy of The Library of Congress.*

Institutes of the Christian Religion

In 1536 John Calvin published the first edition of his major work, *Christianae religionis institutio* (Institutes of the Christian Religion). The book explained the essentials of the Christian faith from a Protestant perspective for common readers, not theologians. Calvin asserted that the only spiritual authority is both the New Testament and the Old Testament (the Christian name for the Hebrew Bible). According to Calvin, the all-knowing and ever-present God had determined, from the beginning of time, who was to be saved and who was to be damned. All people, he felt, were sinful by nature and could never achieve salvation (forgiveness of sins by God) through their own efforts. God had therefore selected a few people, called the "elect," for salvation. The elect were to lead others, who had not been chosen by God, toward salvation. This concept was later called "predestination," but Calvin himself did not use the term. Calvin taught that the purpose of life was to strive to know or understand God as well as possible and then to follow God's will. This could be done only through faith (acceptance of truth without questioning), by which people pursue union with Christ, the embodiment of God on Earth. This faith required them to strive to live a moral life, out of hope that they were among the elect chosen by God. *Institutes* became the most widely read and influential work of theology in the Reformation period.

In 1541 Calvin returned to Geneva in response to a call from the floundering church. He had been assured that he would be given the freedom he felt was necessary to build God's earthly kingdom. He then wrote *Ecclesiastical Ordinances*, which served as the basis of a reorganized local church government to be headed by a group called the consistory. The ordinances were approved by the citizens of Geneva in late 1541.

Things to Remember While Reading Excerpt from *Ecclesiastical Ordinances:*

- In the *Ecclesiastical Ordinances* Calvin established four church offices—minister, teacher, elder, and deacon. Modeled on leaders described in the New Testament (second part of the Bible), these officials were given distinct responsibilities in the new society. Members of the consistory were the ministers of local churches and twelve elders. Calvin set rules for the selection and approval of church officers, specified the times of worship services, and even designated who would attend which church. He also identified unacceptable behavior and defined procedures for dealing with those who broke the rules. Calvin gave the consistory full authority to suppress any opposition to the policies outlined in *Ordinances.*

- Calvin considered himself to be on the side of godliness and truth. Thus, for him, to tolerate dissent of any kind was to tolerate evil. Though Calvin expected strict enforcement of his orders, he was no different from other sixteenth-century reformers. Notice that Huldrych Zwingli, leader of the Protestant movement in Zurich, Switzerland, persecuted, or severely punished, Anabaptists (see **Huldrych Zwingli** entry).

Excerpt from Ecclesiastical Ordinances

On the Frequency, Place, and Time of Preaching

Each Sunday, at daybreak, there shall be a sermon in St. Peter's and St. Gervaise's, also at the customary hour at St. Peter, Magdalene, and St. Gervaise. At three o'clock, as well, in all three parishes, the second sermon.

*For purposes of **catechetical instruction** and the administration of the **sacraments,** the boundaries of all the parishes are to be observed as possible. St. Gervaise is to be used by those who have done so in the past; likewise with Magdalene. Those who formerly attended St. Germaine, Holy Cross, the new church of Our Lady and St. Legier are to attend St. Peter's.*

On work days, besides the two sermons mentioned, there shall be preaching three times each week, on Monday, Wednesday, and Friday. These sermons shall be announced for an early hour so that they may be finished before the day's work begins. On special days of prayer the Sunday order is to be observed.

Catechetical instruction: Teaching of church doctrine in the form of questions and answers.

Sacraments: Holy rites of a church.

To carry out these provisions, and the other responsibilities pertaining to the ministry, five ministers and three **coadjutors** will be needed. The latter will also be ministers and help and reinforce the others as the occasion arises.

Concerning the Second Order, Called Teachers

The proper duty of teachers is to instruct the faithful in sound doctrine so that the purity of the **gospel** is not corrupted by ignorance or evil opinions. We include here the aids and instructions necessary to preserve the doctrines and to keep the church from becoming **desolate** for lack of pastors and ministers. To use a more familiar expression, we shall call it the order of the schools.

The order nearest the ministry and most closely associated with the government of the church is that of lecturer in theology who teaches the Old and New Testament.

Since it is impossible to profit by such instruction without first knowing languages and the **humanities,** and also since it is necessary to prepare for the future in order that the church may not be neglected by the young, it will be necessary to establish a school to instruct the youth, to prepare them not only for the ministry but for government.

First of all, a proper place for teaching purposes must be designated, fit to accommodate children and others who wish to profit by such instruction; to secure someone who is both learned in subject matter and capable of looking after the building, who can also read. This person is to be employed and placed under contract on condition that he provide under his charge readers in the languages and in dialectics, if it be possible. Also to secure men with **bachelor degrees** to teach the children. This we hope to do to further the work of God....

The Third Order Is That of Elders, Those Commissioned or Appointed to the Consistory by the Authorities

Their office is to keep watch over the lives of everyone, to admonish in love those whom they see in error and leading disorderly lives. Whenever necessary they shall make a report concerning these to the ministers who will be designated to make brotherly corrections and join with the others in making such corrections....

The Fourth Order or the Deacons

There were two orders of deacons in the ancient church, the one concerned with receiving, distributing, and guarding the goods of the poor, their possessions, income and pensions as well as the quarterly offerings; the others, to take heed to and care for the sick and

Coadjutors: Assistants.

Gospel: Word of God.

Desolate: Left abandoned.

Humanities: Academic subjects consisting of grammar (rules for the use of a language), rhetoric (art of effective speaking and writing), moral philosophy (study of human conduct and values), poetry, and history.

Bachelor degrees: Certificates showing completion of four years of college.

administer the pittance for the poor. This custom we have preserved to the present. In order to avoid confusion, for we have both **stewards** and managers, one of the four stewards of the hospital is to act as receiver of all goods and is to receive adequate **remuneration** in order that he may better exercise his office....

It will be his task to take **diligent** care that the public hospital is well administered and that it is open not only to the sick but also to aged persons. Those who are sick are to be kept in a separate lodging, away from those who are unable to work, old persons, widows, orphans, and other needy persons....

Above all, the families of the managers are to be well managed in an efficient and godly fashion, since they are to manage the houses dedicated to God....

The hospital, for the **pestilence** in any case, is to be set apart; especially should it happen that the city is visited by this **rod** from God.

Moreover, to prevent begging, which is contrary to good order, it will be necessary that the authorities delegate certain officers. They are to be stationed at the doors of the churches to drive away any who try to resist and, if they act **impudently** or answer **insolently,** to take them to one of the **syndics.** In like manner, the heads of the **precincts** should always watch that the law against begging is well observed.

The Persons Whom the Elders Should Admonish, and Proper Procedure in This Regard

If there shall be anyone who lays down opinions contrary to **received doctrine,** he is to be **summoned.** If he **recants,** he is to be dismissed without prejudice. If he is stubborn, he is to be **admonished** from time to time until it shall be evident that he deserves greater **severity.** Then, he is to be **excommunicated** and this action reported to the **magistrate.**

If anyone is negligent in attending worship so that a noticeable offense is evident for the **communion of the faithful,** or if anyone shows himself **contemptuous** of **ecclesiastical** discipline, he is to be admonished. If he becomes disobedient, he is to be dismissed in love. If he persists, passing from bad to worse, after having been admonished three times, he is to be excommunicated and the matter reported to the authorities.

For the correction of faults, it is necessary to proceed after the **ordinance** of our **Lord.** That is, vices are to be dealt with secretly

Stewards: Those in charge of supplies.

Remuneration: Payment.

Diligent: Earnest.

Pestilence: Epidemic disease.

Rod: Stick used for punishment.

Impudently: Showing disregard for others.

Insolently: Insultingly contemptuous.

Syndics: Representatives of the state.

Precincts: Districts.

Received doctrine: Agreed-upon rules or teachings.

Summoned: Called before the court.

Recants: Confesses sin.

Admonished: Scolded.

Severity: Strict treatment.

Excommunicated: Expelled from church membership.

Magistrate: Judge.

Communion of the faithful: Religious community.

Contemptuous: Scornful

Ecclesiastical: Church.

Ordinance: Stated orders.

Lord: God.

and no one is to be brought before the church for accusation if the fault is neither public nor **scandalous,** unless he has been found rebellious in the matter.

For the rest, those who scorn private admonitions are to be admonished again by the church. If they will not come to reason nor recognize their error, they are to be ordered to **abstain** from **communion** until they improve.

As for obvious and public evil, which the church cannot overlook: if the faults **merit** nothing more than admonition, the duty of the elders shall be to summon those concerned, deal with them in love in order that they may be reformed and, if they correct the fault, to dismiss the matter. If they **persevere,** they are to be admonished again. If, in the end, such procedure proves unsuccessful, they are to be **denounced** as contemptuous of God, and ordered to abstain from communion until it is evident that they have changed their way of life.

As for crimes that merit not only admonition but **punitive** correction: if any fall into error, according to the requirements of the case, it will be necessary to command them to abstain from communion so that they humble themselves before God and repent of their error.

If anyone by being **contumacious** or rebellious attempts that which is forbidden, the duty of the ministers shall be to reject him, since it is not proper that he receive the sacrament.

Nevertheless, let all these measures be moderate; let there not be such a degree of **rigor** that anyone should be cast down, for all corrections are but medicinal, to bring back sinners to the Lord.

And let all be done in such a manner as to keep from the ministers any **civil jurisdiction** whatever, so that they use only the spiritual sword of the word of God as **St. Paul** ordered them. Thus the consistory may in no wise take from the authority of the officers or of civil justice. On the contrary, the civil power is to be kept **intact.** Likewise, when it shall be necessary to exercise punishment or restraint against any party, the ministers and the consistory are to hear the party concerned, deal with them and admonish them as it may seem good, reporting all to the council which, for its part, shall deliberate and then pass judgment according to the **merits** of the case.

Scandalous: Outrageous.

Abstain: Do not participate in.

Communion: Christian ritual in which bread and wine represent the body and blood of Jesus Christ.

Merit: Deserve.

Persevere: Continue.

Denounced: Publicly pronounced to be sinful.

Punitive: Requiring punishment.

Contumacious: Stubbornly disobedient.

Rigor: Strictness.

Civil jurisdiction: Government authority.

St. Paul: Early Christian who founded the first churches.

Intact: Separate.

Merits: Virtues.

What happened next...

Despite considerable opposition, Calvin's influence grew steadily as he defeated theological and political opponents alike. In 1555 the consistory, which acted as a sort of moral court, was accepted and given great powers by the city. From that point onward discipline was strictly enforced in Geneva, which became known as Calvin's "New Jerusalem." Taverns were closed and replaced with *abbayes,* in which patrons were closely scrutinized for signs of excessive drinking. Indeed, throughout Geneva, citizens monitored one another's behavior, ready to report any sort of wrongdoing. In this spirit, a strict moral order—based on Calvin's particular vision of truth—was built. Constantly preaching and writing, he involved himself in all aspects of Genevan affairs including education, trade, diplomacy, and even sanitation. In 1559 Calvin and the French scholar Theodore Beza (1516–1605) founded the Genevan Academy (now the University of Geneva) for the training of clergy. Calvin was also determined to spread the reform movement abroad, especially within his native France. Under his direction, Geneva became a haven for persecuted Protestants. It was also the unofficial center of growing Protestant movements in places as far removed as Scotland. Before Calvin died in1564 he asked Beza to be head of the church of Geneva and help promote Calvinism throughout the world.

Did you know...

- In 1553, Michael Servetus (1511–1553), a Spanish scientist, humanist, and theologian, arrived in Geneva. He was traveling in disguise to avoid persecution for his scandalous religious ideas. Often called the first Unitarian (a present-day Protestant denomination), Servetus denied the divinity, or godliness, of Christ and the doctrine of the Trinity (the Christian concept of God as the Father, the Son, and the Holy Spirit). He believed that God was a single, indivisible divine force. His views alienated him from both Catholics and Protestants. One day Calvin recognized Servetus sitting in the crowd listening to one of his sermons. He promptly had Servetus arrested and put on trial. As the "Defender of the Faith," Calvin demanded Servetus's exe-

Pilgrims worshipping at the Plymouth Colony. The Pilgrims established the colony based on John Calvin's teachings.

cution. His order was supported by the Geneva city government, and on October 27, 1553, Servetus was burned alive for heresy (violation of the laws of God).

• Calvin's teachings were adopted by the Puritans, a strict Protestant group in England. They advocated purification of the Church of England (Anglican Church), the official religion of England. Although the Church of England was considered a Protestant faith, it still practiced many of the teachings and elaborate rituals of the Roman Catholic Church. A few dissenters among the Puritans contended that the church was too corrupt to be saved and they wanted total separation. Separation was considered a crime against the state. Nevertheless, a congregation in Scrooby, England, declared themselves to be Nonconformists, or separatists. When the Scrooby leaders were persecuted in 1607, the congregation went to Leyden in the Netherlands (Holland), where they were free to practice their religion. Eventually they decided to leave the Netherlands and settle in English territory in North America. Calling themselves Pilgrims, they set out aboard a ship called the *Mayflower* in September 1620. Although they were headed for Virginia, a storm forced them into a harbor on the coast of present-day Massachusetts in December 1620. The Pilgrims the established the Plymouth Colony, which was based on the teachings of John Calvin. In 1630 they were joined by other Puritans, who founded the nearby Massachusetts Bay Colony and practiced an even stricter form of Calvinism.

For More Information

Books

Greef, Wulfert de. *The Writings of John Calvin: An Introductory Guide.* Translated by Lyle D. Bierma. Grand Rapids, Mich.: Baker Books, 1993.

Parker, T. H. L. *John Calvin, a Biography.* Philadelphia: Westminster Press, 1975.

Web Sites

"Calvin, John." *Encyclopedia.com.* [Online] Available http://www.encyclopedia.com/searchpool.asp?target=@DOCTITLE%20Calvin%20%20John, April 10, 2002.

Elizabeth

*Excerpt from "Elizabeth, A Dutch Anabaptist martyr:
a letter" (1573)*

Reprinted in *The Protestant Reformation*

Edited by Hans J. Hillerbrand
Published in 1968

In the early 1500s reformers began calling for changes within the Roman Catholic Church, which was the only established Christian religion in Europe at that time. An organized
reform movement began after 1517, when the German theology professor (one who teaches religion) **Martin Luther**
(1483–1546; see entry) posted his grievances against the
church at Wittenberg, Germany. Support of Luther's ideas
gained momentum, eventually resulting in the Protestant Reformation and the establishment of Protestantism as a separate Christian faith. Simultaneously, reform efforts known as
the Catholic Reformation (also the Counter Reformation)
were taking place within the **Roman Catholic Church** (see
entry). In 1555, following a series of conflicts between
Catholics and Protestants in Germany, the Peace of Augsburg
stated that each of more than three hundred principalities in
Germany would adopt the religion of its local ruler. This left
more than half of Germany to Lutherans, the name given to
supporters of Luther's teachings.

Since the earliest stage of the Protestant Reformation,
however, there had been disharmony among Protestants. All

Protestants did not consider themselves Lutherans. Going far beyond the grievances listed by Luther—who never sought complete separation from the church—the Swiss reformer **Huldrych Zwingli** (1484–1531; see entry) abandoned Lutheranism in the early 1520s and promoted his own brand of Protestantism in Switzerland. The French-born Swiss reformer **John Calvin** (1504–1564; see entry) also did not agree with many of Luther's ideas. Beginning in the late 1540s, from his base in Basel, Switzerland, Calvin advocated an even stricter form of Protestantism called Calvinism. The teachings of Zwingli, and particularly those of Calvin, were adopted elsewhere in Europe, but they did not necessarily reflect the views of everyone who claimed to be a Protestant. In fact, the Protestant movement was virtually in disarray, especially after the Peace of Augsburg, as hundreds of new radical Protestant sects (small groups with extreme views) were constantly forming and re-forming. Many of these sects had roots in the first phase of the Reformation. One of the strongest was the Anabaptists.

Swiss Brethren dispute baptism

The Anabaptist movement, first known as the Swiss Brethren, arose in the early 1520s among Zwingli's followers in Switzerland, then spread into Germany and the Netherlands. In 1527 the Swiss Brethren issued a statement of their beliefs in the Schleitheim Confession. Differences between the Brethren and mainstream Protestants focused on the question of baptism. Baptism is a Christian rite in which a person is anointed with water and accepted into the Christian faith. Like the Catholics, most Protestants believed in baptizing infants in order to assure that a new life would be set on the path of God. The Brethren, on the other hand, contended that a person should be baptized in adulthood even if he or she had been baptized as an infant. They referred to their form of baptism as believer's baptism because it was the voluntary choice of a mature person who was ready to accept Christianity. A member of the Swiss Brethren came to be known as an "Anabaptist," the word for "one who baptizes again." Lutherans and Calvinists often used "Anabaptist" as a negative term for any sect that did not follow standard reform practices. Like the Calvinists and the Lutherans, the Anabaptists stressed the importance of personal communication with God, and they rejected the rituals of the Catholic Church. They were different from other Protestant groups, however, because they advocated nonviolence, opposed state churches, did not participate in state government, and refused to take oaths.

Anabaptism was embraced mainly by the poor and by uneducated peasants and artisans. Anabaptists were seen as a threat by the Zwinglians. In 1525 a dispute between the two groups led to the suppression of the Anabaptist movement in Zurich and later to the banishment of its members. They were prosecuted, and in 1527 one of their leaders, Felix Mantz, was among those executed. Wherever Anabaptists and other radical sects went in Europe, they encountered similar persecution, or punishment for their beliefs. They were targeted by both Protestant and Catholic government authorities, who disapproved of their community-based doctrines and their opposition to state churches. Seldom free to practice their religion, radicals risked being arrested and put in prison, and they were often burned at the stake. (It was believed that burning was a way to destroy evil spirits.) Government authorities argued that such harsh measures had to be taken because radicals were heretics (those who violated the laws of God) who posed a threat to law and order.

So many Anabaptists were executed that they soon came to be regarded as martyrs (those who set an example by sacrificing their lives for their beliefs). In the seventeenth century Thieleman van Braght, a Dutchman, collected documents relating to Anabaptist martyrs in a book titled *The Bloody Theater of the Martyrs' Mirror*. Among the documents was a letter a Dutch Anabaptist woman named Elizabeth (her last name is unknown) wrote to her infant daughter Janneken. Following is an excerpt from Elizabeth's letter.

Things to Remember While Reading an Excerpt from "Elizabeth, A Dutch Anabaptist martyr: a letter":

- Elizabeth wrote the letter in 1573 from a prison in Antwerp (a city in present-day Belgium), shortly after giving birth to Janneken. Elizabeth's husband had already been executed, and she herself was about to meet the same fate. She was leaving the letter for Janneken, both as

a remembrance of herself and her husband and as a guide for her daughter's moral and spiritual development.

- Notice that Elizabeth is willingly sacrificing her life as a way to spread the message of Christ (the name for Jesus of Nazareth, the founder of Christianity). She tells Janneken not to be ashamed of her parents because they were following the example of Christ and the early Christians (the prophets and apostles), who were also persecuted. In fact, Elizabeth feels that she has been chosen by Christ, who said, "Ye shall be persecuted, killed, and dispersed for my name's sake."

- Throughout the letter Elizabeth refers to important figures in the Christian religion. "Father" and "Lord" are terms for God. Abraham, Jacob, and Isaac were Hebrew patriarchs (fathers of the Hebrew people) who appear in the Old Testament (first part of the Bible, the Christian holy book; also called the Hebrew Bible). Abraham was

A mass baptism of Anabaptists in a river. Unlike the Catholic Church and other Protestant religions, the Anabaptists believed that a person should be baptized in adulthood instead of being baptized as an infant. *Reproduced by permission of Mary Evans Picture Library.*

the first prophet and founder of the Hebrew nation. Isaac was the son of Abraham and is revered as the second Hebrew prophet. Jacob, the Lord in Israel, was the son of Isaac. He was given the name Israel ("Prince of God") by Jehovah (the Hebrew term for God).

- Elizabeth also quotes passages from the Bible. Matt. 6:33 is the book of Matthew, chapter 6, verse 33. The second epistle (2 Thess. 3:10) of Paul (founder of first Christian churches) is to the Thessalonians, chapter 3, verse 10, and I Peter 3:10 is the first epistle of Peter (leader of Christianity after the death of Christ), chapter 3, verse 10. Matthew, 2 Thessalonians, and 1 Peter are all books of the New Testament, the second part of the Bible, which contains the teachings of Christ.

Excerpt from "Elizabeth, A Dutch Anabaptist martyr: a letter"

[Testament] written to Janneken my own dearest daughter, while I was (unworthily) confined for the Lord's sake, in prison, at Antwerp, A.D. 1573.

*The true love of God and wisdom of the Father strengthen you in virtue, my dearest child; the Lord of heaven and earth, the God of Abraham, the God of Isaac, and the God of Jacob, the Lord in Israel, keep you in His virtue, and strengthen and confirm your understanding in His truth. My dear little child, I commend you to the almighty, great and terrible God, who only is wise, that He will keep you, and let you grow up in His fear, or that He will take you home in your youth, this is my heart's request of the Lord: you who are yet so young, and whom I must leave here in this wicked, evil, **perverse** world.*

*Since, then, the Lord has so ordered and **foreordained** it, that I must leave you here, and you are here deprived of father and mother, I will **commend** you to the Lord; let Him do with you according to His holy will. He will govern you, and be a Father to you, so that you shall have no lack here, if you only fear God; for He will be the Father of the orphans and the Protector of the widows.*

Perverse: Turned away from what is right or good.

Foreordained: Decided in advance.

Commend: Place in the care of.

Hence, my dear lamb, I who am imprisoned and bound here for the Lord's sake, can help you in no other way; I had to leave your father for the Lord's sake, and could keep him only a short time. We were permitted to live together only half a year, after which we were **apprehended,** *because we sought the* **salvation** *of our souls. They took him from me, not knowing my condition [her pregnancy], and I had to remain in imprisonment, and see him go before me; and it was a great grief to him, that I had to remain here in prison. And now that I have abided the time, and borne you under my heart with great sorrow for nine months, and given birth to you here in prison, in great pain, they have taken you from me. Here I lie, expecting death every morning, and shall now soon follow your dear father. And I, your dear mother, write you, my dearest child, something for a remembrance, that you will thereby remember your dear father and your dear mother.*

Since I am now delivered up to death, and must leave you here alone, I must through these lines cause you to remember, that when you have attained your understanding, you endeavor to fear God, and see and examine why and for whose name we both died; and be not ashamed to confess us before the world, for you must know that it is not for the sake of any evil. Hence be not ashamed of us; it is the way which the prophets and the apostles went, and the narrow way which leads into eternal life, for there shall no other way be found by which to be saved.

Hence, my young lamb, for whose sake I still have, and have had, great sorrow, seek, when you have attained your understanding, this narrow way, though there is sometimes much danger in it according to the flesh, as we may see and read, if we **diligently** *examine and read the* **Scriptures,** *that much is said concerning the* **cross of Christ.** *And there are many in this world who are enemies of the cross, who seek to be free from it among the world, and to escape it. But, my dear child, if we would with Christ seek and inherit salvation, we must also help bear His cross; and this is the cross which He would have us bear: to follow His footsteps, and to help bear His* **reproach;** *for Christ Himself says: "Ye shall be persecuted, killed, and dispersed for my name's sake." Yea, He Himself went before us in this way of reproach, and left us an example, that we should follow His steps; for, for His sake all must be* **forsaken,** *father, mother, sister, brother, husband, child, yea, one's own life....*

Thus, my dear child, it is now fulfilled in your dear father and mother. It was indeed **prophesied** *to us beforehand, that this was*

Apprehended: Captured.

Salvation: Deliverance from sin.

Diligently: Earnestly and energetically.

Scriptures: Text of the Bible.

Cross of Christ: Symbol of Christianity; Christ was executed by being hung on a cross.

Reproach: Express displeasure with.

Forsaken: Turned away from.

Prophesied: Predicted with assurance on the basis of mystical knowledge.

*awaiting us; but not everyone is chosen **hereunto,** nor expects it; the Lord has chosen us hereunto. Hence, when you have **attained** your understanding, follow this example of your father and mother. And, my dear child, this is my request of you, since you are still very little and young; I wrote this when you were but one month old. As I am soon now to offer up my sacrifice, by the help of the Lord, I leave you this: "That you fulfil my request, always uniting with them that fear God; and do not regard the **pomp** and boasting of the world, nor the great **multitude,** whose way leads to the **abyss of hell,** but look at the little flock of **Israelites,** who have no freedom anywhere, and must always flee from one land to the other, as Abraham did; that you may hereafter obtain your fatherland; for if you seek your salvation, it is easy to perceive which is the way that leads to life, or the way that leads into hell. Above all things, seek the kingdom of heaven and His righteousness; and whatever you need besides shall be added unto you." Matt. 6:33.*

Further, my dear child, I pray you, that wherever you live when you are grown up, and begin to have understanding, you conduct yourself well and honestly, so that no one need have cause to complain of you. And always be faithful, taking good heed not to wrong any one. Learn to carry your hands always uprightly, and see that you like to work, for Paul says: "If any will not work, neither shall he eat." 2 Thess. 3:10. And Peter says: "He that will love life, and see good days, let him refrain his tongue from evil." I Pet. 3:10.

What happened next...

In spite of persecution, the Anabaptists and other radicals were important to the Protestant Reformation. Many of these religious groups were headed by lay, or unordained, preachers who came to see the close connections among religion, politics, and economics. They continued pressing for social and political reforms, which they justified with passages from the Bible. The Reformation thus spread to all aspects of life, and the Christian world found itself in the middle of the most profound upheaval since Roman Catholicism was founded around C.E. 600. By the close of the Protestant Reformation in the early seventeenth century, the Christian

Hereunto: To this.

Attained: Achieved.

Pomp: Show of magnificence.

Multitude: Majority of people.

Abyss of hell: Bottomless pit of the place where sinners go after death.

Israelites: People of Israel.

world was divided into five factions—Catholic, Lutheran, Calvinist, Anglican (Church of England), and Anabaptist. Within this structure new sects continued to emerge, and many still exist today. In fact, the Anabaptists were the forerunners of the modern Baptists, one of the largest Protestant denominations in the world.

Did you know...

- Closely related to the Anabaptists were the Hutterites (Moravian Brethren), a group founded by Jakob Hutter, an Austrian pacifist (one who is opposed to violence). The Hutterites established communities based on mutual Christian love and the sharing of goods. Another prominent Anabaptist group was the Mennonites. They were led by the Dutch reformer Menno Simons (c. 1496–1561), a well-known Anabaptist theologian. Simons stressed the importance of living according to the teachings of Christ.

Like the Hutterites, the Mennonites formed close-knit communities that lived apart from the rest of the world. Today Hutterites and Mennonites continue to live in Europe and North America.

• Many other sects were formed during the Protestant Reformation. Among them were the Spiritualists, who sought personal communion with the Holy Spirit (the third person of the Holy Trinity). The Evangelical Rationalists and Puritans of both Poland and England applied "right reason" to such concepts as the deity (godliness) of Christ, the Trinity (the Christian idea of God as the Father, Son, and Holy Spirit), and the existence of heaven and hell (places where the saved and sinners, respectively, go after death). The Levellers and True Levellers, Ranters, Seekers, Muggletonians, Antinomians, and scores of other radical groups rose up, especially in England, Belgium, and France. They came to be known by both Catholics and conservative Protestants as "the lunatic fringe."

For More Information

Books

Anthony, Arthur. *The Tailor-King: The Rise and Fall of the Anabaptist Kingdom of Münster.* New York: St. Martin's Press, 1989.

Hillerbrand, Hans J., ed. *The Protestant Reformation.* New York: Harper Torchbooks, 1968.

Loewen, Harry, and Steven M. Nolt. *Through Fire & Water: An Overview of Mennonite History.* Scottdale, Pa.: Herald Press, 1996.

Video Recordings

The Radicals. Worcester, Pa.: Gateway Films-Vision Video, 1989.

Web Sites

The Schleitheim Confession. [Online] Available http://www.anabaptists.org/history/schleith.html, April 10, 2002.

Catholic Reformation

5

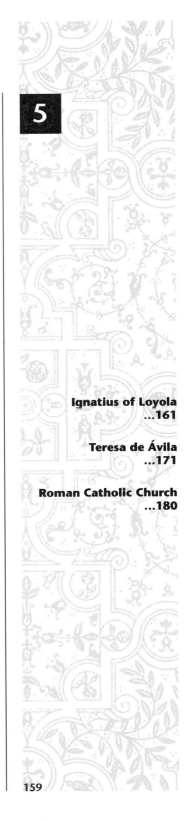

The Catholic Reformation officially began when the Council of Trent was convened in 1545. Prior to that time, however, priests, nuns, bishops, and popes had been trying to bring about reform. Among them was the Spanish priest Ignatius of Loyola, who founded the Society of Jesus (Jesuits) in 1540. The foundation of the Jesuit's practices was Ignatius's numerous notes on ways to become a more devout Christian. Later titled *Spiritual Exercises,* the book became highly influential within the church. Another reformer was the Spanish nun Teresa de Ávila, who is credited with reviving Catholicism in the 1560s and 1570s, when Protestantism threatened to bring down the church. Her most significant contribution was the founding of the Reformed Discalced (Barefoot) Carmelite Convent of San Jose, a Catholic order for women. Teresa is best known today as one of the great Catholic mystics. Teresa had many mystical experiences, called raptures, which she described in several books. Among her most widely read works is *The Life of Teresa of Jesus.*

Reforms within the Catholic Church were also initiated by the Council of Trent, a conference of church officials.

The Council of Trent completed its work in 1563 and issued a report titled *Canons and Degrees of the Council of Trent.* The following year Pope Pius IV released the Profession of the Tridentine Faith, which was a binding creed for teachers of church doctrines. The Profession was a summary of the major decisions of the Council of Trent as reported in *Canons and Decrees.* Although no Protestants were mentioned by name in these documents, Protestant teachings were discussed by the council. The Profession of the Tridentine Faith therefore reflected the church's response to the main points of contention between Catholics and Protestants.

Ignatius of Loyola

Excerpt from Spiritual Exercises *(1548)*
Reprinted in *The Spiritual Exercises of St. Ignatius*
Translated by Louis J. Puhl
Published in 2000

During the sixteenth and seventeenth centuries a reform movement called the Catholic Reformation took place within the Roman Catholic Church. The reform effort is also frequently called the Counter Reformation, but many historians prefer not to use this term. It suggests that changes within the church were simply a reaction to the Protestant Reformation, the reform movement started in 1517 by the German priest **Martin Luther** (see entry). In fact, many Catholics were already aware that reform was needed as early as the fifteenth century, one hundred years before Protestants left the church and formed a separate Christian religion. By that time popes (supreme heads of the church), cardinals (officials ranking directly below the pope), bishops (heads of church districts), and priests (pastors of congregations) had become corrupt and greedy. Neglecting their responsibilities as spiritual leaders, they pursued their own personal advancement. The church had accumulated more property and wealth than kings and princes. Many Catholics, both inside and outside the church, were troubled by this situation.

Popes showed no serious interest in reform, however, until 1537, when Pope Paul III (1468–1549; reigned 1534–49) appointed a committee of cardinals to study problems in the church. Their report, *A Council ... for Reforming the Church,* denounced evils and abuses at all levels. Most of these abuses were laid at the door of the papacy (office of the pope) itself. For the next few years Pope Paul tried to convene a council, but it had to be postponed several times. The first session of a council of bishops finally met at Trent in northern Italy in 1545. Known as the Council of Trent, it is considered the beginning of the Catholic Reformation.

In the meantime Pope Paul had initiated his own reforms and encouraged many new religious communities. Among them was the Society of Jesus (known as the Jesuits), which the pope approved in 1540. The Jesuit order was led by Ignatius Loyola (1491–1556), a nobleman from the Basque region of northern Spain. Baptized Iñigo de Oñaz y Loyola, he adopted the name Ignatius in about 1537, in honor of Saint Ignatius of Antioch, an early church martyr (one who sacrifices his or her life for a cause). After receiving a limited education, he became a soldier. His brief military career ended in 1521 when he was wounded in battle at Pamplona, Spain, during the Italian Wars (a conflict between Spain and France over control of Italy; 1494–1559). While Ignatius was recuperating, he had a series of religious experiences that changed the course of his life. He began a program of asceticism (strict self-denial) for which his Jesuit followers later honored him, and he decided to devote his life to the poor.

Ignatius starts Jesuits

During this time Ignatius tried to confess and do penance (show sorrow or repentance) for all the sins of his earlier life. When he found he had committed so many sins that he could not enumerate them, a priest suggested writing them out. Over the next twenty years Ignatius took a large number of notes on ways to become a more devout Christian. In 1524 he took a pilgrimage, or religious journey, to Jerusalem, the holy city of Christians in Israel (called the Holy Land). Upon his return Ignatius decided he needed a better education if he was to do his work effectively. He studied Latin at Barcelona, and then moved in 1526 to the recently founded university at Alcalá de Henares. Finally he spent a short time at the University of Salamanca. While Ignatius was at Alcalá de Henares and Salamanca, Catholic officials suspected him of being involved in Luther's reform movement. Holy Roman Emperor Charles V (1500–1558; ruled 1519–56), who was also the king of Spain, was unable to stop the spread of Luther's ideas (called Lutheranism) in Germany. To stamp out Lutheranism in Spain, Charles used the Spanish Inquisition, a church court established in the 1490s to find and punish heretics (those who violate laws of God and the church). Although Ignatius does not appear to have known about Luther, he was imprisoned without trial or formal charges on several occasions. He always insisted on a judgment, but he was usually found blameless despite his unconventional practices. In 1528 Ignatius went to the University of Paris, which was then the center of Catholic learning in Europe.

Ignatius of Loyola, founder of the Jesuits.
©Bettmann/Corbis.
Reproduced by permission of Corbis Corporation.

While in Paris, Ignatius met six of the men who were to form the nucleus of the Jesuits. Ignatius was ordained a priest in 1537. He then received permission from Pope Paul III for his group to make a pilgrimage to Jerusalem, where he hoped they might remain as hospital workers. They planned to take a ship from the port of Venice to Syria, but Turkish pirates (ship robbers) in the Mediterranean Sea prevented any pilgrim ships from setting sail that year. This was the only year in the past half century that pilgrim ships did not leave Venice. The "Company of Jesus," as they now called themselves, took it as a warning that their future work did not lie in the Holy Land. Ignatius invited his companions from around Italy to join him in Rome. The time had come, he told them, to establish an order that differed from the older orders of the church (Benedictines, Carthusians, Franciscans, Dominicans, and others).

Ignatius and his followers established rules for their new group. First, they would be loyal to the pope. Second, they would not live a monastic life with regular hours of prayer and choral singing. Third, strict obedience to leaders of the order would be the foremost priority. Members were to be made strong and adaptable through prayer, self-surrender, and a very long training period. In 1541 Ignatius was named the first superior general of the Jesuits.

The basis of the practices of the Jesuit order was the notes Ignatius had been taking for more than two decades. As the order increased in size, the Jesuits began sharing the notes and copies were printed twice in Spanish for distribution. In 1548 Ignatius anonymously published a Latin version with the pope's approval. Titled *Spiritual Exercises,* the book became highly influential within the church. The exercises are still followed by Catholics today.

Things to Remember While Reading an Excerpt from *Spiritual Exercises:*

- *Spiritual Exercises* outlines a thirty-day regimen (systematic plan) of prayer and self-abasement (acts of self-denial and punishment), with the understanding that devotion to God must be central. It is to be used as a handbook by the director of a retreat, a period of time set aside for contemplation and spiritual renewal. *Spiritual Exercises* is intended for one person who goes into retreat for a month, avoiding contact with the outside world. The person meets with the director several times a day to discuss his or her spiritual progress. As in Ignatius's own time, the exercises are often administered to groups, and to lay persons (unordained church members) as well as priests. Ignatius gave specific instructions for modifying the exercises according to the needs of a particular person. For instance, beginners should go through only the first exercise. Some people may not be able to go into complete seclusion, so a director can extend the exercises over a longer period of time.

- The book starts with general observations, directions, rules, and notes, which provide a frame of reference for the exercises. The purpose is to help the person seeking spiritual renewal to overcome lack of discipline and make a firmer commitment to God and to Christ's teachings.

- The exercises are divided into four "weeks," or segments. The first week is a time of conversion from a life of sin to observance of God's commandments. The second week is devoted to committing oneself to the service of others through imitation of Christ. The third week involves identifying with Christ's suffering, and the fourth week concludes with a joyful communion with the risen Christ. (According to Christian tradition, Jesus arose from the dead after being crucified.)

- The first exercise from *Spiritual Exercises* is excerpted below.

Excerpt from Spiritual Exercises

45. *FIRST EXERCISE*

*This is a meditation on the first, second, and third sin employing the three powers of the soul. After the preparatory prayer and two **preludes** it contains three principal points and a **colloquy***

46. PRAYER. In the preparatory prayer I will beg God our Lord for grace that all my intentions, actions, and operations may be directed purely to the praise and service of His Divine Majesty.

47. FIRST PRELUDE. This is mental representation of the place.

*Attention must be called to the following point. When the contemplation or meditation is on something visible, for example, when we contemplate Christ our Lord, the representation will consist in seeing in imagination the material place where the object is that we wish to contemplate. I said the material place, for example, the temple, or the mountain where Jesus or **His Mother** is, according to the subject matter of the contemplation.*

*In a case where the subject matter is not visible, as here in a meditation on sin, the representation will be to see in imagination my soul as a prisoner in this **corruptible** body, and to consider my whole composite being as an **exile** here on earth, cast out to live among brute beasts. I said my whole composite being, body and soul.*

Preludes: Introductory actions.

Colloquy: Conversation.

His Mother: Mary; also known as the Virgin Mary.

Corruptible: Capable of being changed from good to bad.

Exile: Forced absence from one's home or country.

48. THE SECOND PRELUDE. I will ask God our Lord for what I want and desire.

The **petition** made in this prelude must be according to the subject matter. Thus in a contemplation on the **Resurrection** I will ask for joy with Christ in joy. In one on the **passion**, I will ask for sorrow, tears, and anguish with Christ in anguish.

Here it will be to ask for shame and confusion, because I see how many have been lost on account of a single **mortal sin**, and how many times I have deserved eternal **damnation**, because of the many **grievous sins** that I have committed.

49. Note

The Preparatory Prayer, which is never changed, and the two Preludes mentioned above, which are changed at times according to the subject matter, must always be made before all the contemplations and meditations.

*50. THE FIRST POINT. This will consist in using the memory to recall the first sin, which was that of the **angels**, and then in applying the understanding by reasoning upon this sin, then the will by seeking to remember and understand all to be the more filled with shame and confusion when I compare the one sin of the angels with the many sins I have committed. I will consider that they went to **hell** for one sin, and the number of times I have deserved to be condemned forever because of my numerous sins.*

I said we should apply the memory to the sin of the angels, that is, recalling that they were created in the state of grace, that they did not want to make use of the freedom God gave them to reverence and obey their Creator and Lord, and so falling into pride, were changed from grace to hatred of God, and cast out of **heaven** into hell.

So, too, the understanding is to be used to think over the matter more in detail, and then the will to rouse more deeply the emotions.

*51. SECOND POINT. In the same way the three powers of the soul are to be applied to the sin of **Adam and Eve**. Recall to memory how on account of this sin they did penance for so long a time, and the great corruption which came upon the human race that caused so many to be lost in hell.*

I said recall to mind the second sin, that of our First Parents. After Adam had been created on the **Plain of Damascus** and placed in the **Garden of Paradise**, and Eve had been formed from

---

Petition: Request.

Resurrection: Rising of Christ from the dead.

Passion: The sufferings of Christ between the Last Supper and his death.

Mortal sin: Crime against God that results in the soul going to hell.

Damnation: Condemned to hell.

Grievous sins: Serious crimes against God.

Angels: Spiritual beings superior to humans.

Hell: Place where unsaved souls go after death.

Heaven: Place where saved souls go after death.

Adam and Eve: The first man and woman on Earth in the book of Genesis, chapter 2, of the Bible.

Plain of Damascus: An area in present-day Syria.

Garden of Paradise: Garden of Eden.

Renaissance and Reformation: Primary Sources

his side, they sinned by violating the command not to eat of the tree of knowledge. Thereafter, they were clothed in garments of skin and cast out of Paradise. By their sin they lost original justice, and for the rest of their lives, lived without it in many labors and great penance.

So, too, the understanding is to be used to think over the matter in greater detail, and the will is to be used as explained above.

52. THIRD POINT. In like manner, we are to do the same with regard to the third sin, namely, that of one who went to hell because of one mortal sin. Consider also countless others who have been lost for fewer sins than I have committed.

*I said to do the same for the third particular sin. Recall to memory the **gravity** and **malice** of sin against our Creator and Lord. Use the understanding to consider that because of sin, and of acting against the Infinite Goodness, one is justly **condemned** forever. Close with the acts of the will as we have said above.*

53. COLLOQUY. Imagine Christ our Lord present before you upon the cross, and begin to speak with him, asking how it is that though He is the Creator, He has stooped to become man, and to pass from eternal life to death here in time, that thus He might die for our sins.

I shall also reflect upon myself and ask:

"What have I done for Christ?"

"What am I doing for Christ?"

"What ought I to do for Christ?"

As I behold Christ in this plight, nailed to the cross, I shall ponder upon what presents itself to my mind.

What happened next...

Ignatius's order eventually attracted more than a thousand members. Several Jesuits acted as experts at the Council of Trent. The Jesuits also moved early into the field of education, founding colleges in Italy, Portugal, the Netherlands, Spain, Germany, and India. These colleges became the basis of the Jesuit educational system that has continued to

Gravity: Seriousness.

Malice: Ill will.

Condemned: Judged guilty.

the present. Ignatius died in 1556, and he was declared a saint in 1622. By that time the Jesuits had become the single most powerful weapon of the Catholic Reformation.

Did you know...

- Ignatius ruined his health with his strict ascetic practices. He sometimes went days at a time without food, walked barefoot in winter, and deliberately neglected his long hair until it was matted and filthy. He wore a hair shirt (garment made of rough animal hair worn next to the skin) and sometimes a nail-studded belt turned inward to his body. These torments weakened him and gave him a pale and haggard appearance, which terrified both strangers and acquaintances. He also had lifelong stomach problems. In his last fifteen years he worked a twenty-hour day, resting only to recover from increasingly severe illnesses. Ignatius died in 1556 after a day of hard work.

- After Ignatius of Loyola, perhaps the most famous Jesuit was Francis Xavier (1506–1552). One of the six original followers of Ignatius, he was born into a noble family at the castle of Xavier in the kingdom of Navarre (a region between France and Spain). In 1542 Ignatius chose Francis to go to India. For seven years Francis ministered to Portuguese settlers and newly converted Indians. He reportedly baptized more than ten thousand people in Travancore (a region in southwest India) alone. He also did mission work in Malaysia, Indonesia, and the Spice Islands. In 1549 he became the first Catholic missionary to Japan, where he wrote a Japanese catechism (religious instruction in the form of questions and answers) in the Latin alphabet. In 1551 Francis became head of Jesuit missions in the region from the Cape of Good Hope (an extension of land at the tip of South Africa) to China and Japan. During his work in Asia, Francis emphasized that it was essential for missionaries to learn the languages and customs of the people they hoped to convert. He also advocated training native people as clergymen. He became ill and died while trying to make a secret trip into China. Francis was declared a saint in 1622, and in 1927 Pope Pius XI named him patron of all missions.

For More Information

Books

Ignatius of Loyola. *The Spiritual Exercises of St. Ignatius.* Translated by Louis J. Puhl. New York: Vintage Books, 2000.

Olin, John C., ed. *The Autobiography of St. Ignatius Loyola.* Translated by Joseph F. O'Callaghan. New York: Fordham University Press, 1993.

O'Malley, John W. *The First Jesuits.* Cambridge, Mass.: Harvard University Press, 1993.

Purcell, Mary. *The First Jesuit, St. Ignatius Loyola (1491–1556).* Chicago: Loyola University Press, 1981.

Web Sites

Knight, Kevin. "St. Ignatius Loyola." *Catholic Encyclopedia.* [Online] Available http://www.newadvent.org/cathen/07639c.htm, April 10, 2002.

"Loyola, Saint Ignatius of." *Bitannica.com.* [Online] Available http://www.britannica.com/eb/article?eu=50361&tocid=0&query=ignatius%20loyola, April 10, 2002.

The Spiritual Exercises of St. Ignatius of Loyola. Translated from the autograph by Father Elder Mullan, S.J. [Online] Available http://www.ccel.org/i/ignatius/exercises/exercises.html, April 10, 2002.

Teresa de Ávila

Excerpt from **The Life of Teresa of Jesus** *(1611)*
Translated by E. Allison Peers
Published in 1960

The Spanish religious reformer Teresa de Ávila (Teresa of Jesus; 1515–1582) was an important figure in the Catholic Reformation (also called the Counter Reformation), a reform movement within the Roman Catholic Church that took place in the sixteenth and seventeenth centuries (see **Roman Catholic Church** entry). The Roman Catholic Church is a Christian religion based in Rome, Italy, and headed by a pope. When the Catholic Reformation began in the mid-1500s, Catholicism was still the only established Christian religion in the Western (non-Asian) world. Nevertheless, the stability of the church was being threatened by the Protestant Reformation, a widespread reform movement in central Europe that was started by the German theology professor (teacher of religion) Martin Luther in 1517 (see **Martin Luther** entry). By the end of the sixteenth century Protestants had formed their own Christian denominations (church groups), which were separate from the Catholic Church. Teresa is credited with reviving Catholicism in the 1560s and 1570s when Protestantism threatened to bring down the church. Her most significant contribution was the founding of the Reformed Discalced (Barefoot) Carmelite Convent of San Jose, a Catholic order for women. At the time of her death in 1582 she had started seventeen new Reformed Discalced Carmelite convents, or religious houses, in Spain.

Teresa is best known today as one of the great Catholic mystics (those who believe in direct knowledge of God through intense spiritual experience). She had many mystical experiences, called raptures, which she described in several books. Among her most widely read works is her autobiography, *The Life of Teresa of Jesus* (1611).

Teresa joins Carmelites

Teresa was born Teresa de Cepeda y Ahumada in 1515 on a farm near Ávila, Spain. Her father was Alonso (Pina) de Cepeda, son of a wealthy Jewish businessman who had converted to Christianity, and her mother was Beatriz de Ahumada, a farmer's daughter. When Teresa was fourteen she entered Our Lady of Grace convent, where she remained until she became ill with a weak heart in 1532. She also suffered from rheumatoid arthritis (painful inflammation and swelling of the joints) for the rest of her life. After recuperating for nearly three years, she decided to become a nun. One of her greatest fears was going to hell (the place where sinners go after death) when she died, and she wanted to be a nun because of that fear. Her father disapproved of her decision, so she ran away to the Carmelite Convent of the Encarnacion (Incarnation) in Ávila. She became a nun in 1537 and took the name of Teresa de Jesus. The convent, which was uncloistered (nuns were not required to stay inside), offered great freedom to the Carmelites. They wore perfume, jewelry, and colorful sashes. Later, Teresa called it "an inn just off the road of hell." While living at the convent she met a nobleman and fell in love, an experience that was deeply disturbing to her. About a year later she became ill again and left the Carmelites. While recovering at her sister's home she began reading books on "mystical theology," a religious philosophy based on intense spiritual experiences. Teresa rejoined the Carmelites around 1540 and spent the next three years, as she put it in *Life,* "from pastime to pastime, from vanity to vanity, from occasion to occasion."

In 1543, Teresa's father died and she went through a long struggle with inner conflicts. Although she suffered over the next ten years, the people around her saw her as a "distin-

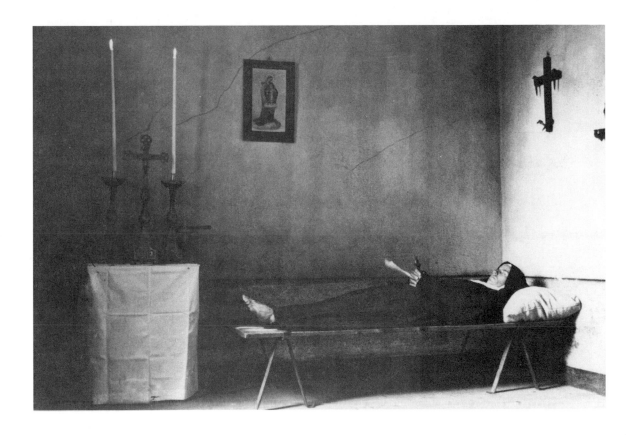

guished lady" who was "gay and witty." Teresa agonized over her feelings for men, especially a nobleman and priest named Garcia de Toledo. In 1554 she experienced a conversion, or spiritual change, when she saw a statue of the wounded Jesus of Nazareth (called Christ), the founder of Christianity. Then someone gave her a copy of *Confessions* by Saint Augustine (354–430), an early church leader. She identified with the spiritual suffering described by Augustine and realized that she was not destined for eternal suffering in hell. The following year she asked for permission to leave the convent. Her request was granted because her practices in penance (seeking forgiveness for sin) and prayer were considered extreme, compared to the casual lifestyle of the Carmelites. She went to live with a friend and spent her time reading. In 1557, Pope Paul IV established the Index of Forbidden Books, a list of works that the Roman Catholic Church considered to be heretical (in violation of the laws of God and the church). Many mystical books were on the list, so Teresa could not continue her study of mystical theology. In 1559, her book collection was burned by judges of the Spanish Inquisition, a church court established for the purpose of finding and punishing heretics.

Life is criticized by the church

Teresa had been writing *Life,* and she completed the book in 1562. Since mystical works had been banned, the Inquisition judges ordered her to expand the manuscript by filling in facts about her visions. Many times she fell into seizures, or trancelike states, and did not remember what had happened. Witnesses described these events, and gossip had spread throughout the community. Teresa claimed to hear voices and see visions of both the devil (figure who represents evil) and Christ. As a result of these visions, many people thought she was possessed by the devil and should be exorcised (a ritual in which a priest drives out evil spirits). According to some accounts, Teresa also experienced levitation (lifting of the body by supernatural forces). She did not want church officials to know about her visions because inquisitors were searching for heretics and burning them at the stake. She feared that inquisitors would think she was making a pact with the devil and would convict her of heresy. Teresa completed her expanded version of *Life* in 1565 and it was accepted by the inquisitors. (The church did not approve the publication of any of Teresa's works until 1588, six years after her death. *Life* was published in 1611.)

Things to Remember While Reading an Excerpt from *The Life of Teresa of Jesus:*

- One of Teresa's greatest fears was going to hell when she died, and she decided to become a nun because of that fear. In this excerpt she vividly described a terrible vision in which she was plunged directly into hell. She believed it was the Lord's (God's) will that she visit this place so she would know the punishment awaiting sinners. The experience left her determined not to sin again.

- Notice that Teresa mentioned Lutherans in the last paragraph. "Lutheran" was the name for followers of Martin

Luther; they were also known as Protestants. Teresa singled out Lutherans as being destined for hell because they had been baptized as Catholics and were committing heresy by challenging the church.

Excerpt from
The Life of Teresa of Jesus

I was at prayer one day when suddenly, without knowing how, I found myself, as I thought, plunged right into hell. I realized that it was the Lord's will that I should see the place which the devils had prepared for me there and which I had merited for my sins. This happened in the briefest space of time, but, even if I were to live for many years, I believe it would be impossible for me to forget it. The entrance, I thought, resembled a very long, narrow passage, like a furnace, very low, dark and closely confined; the ground seemed to be full of water which looked like filthy, evil-smelling mud, and in it were many wicked-looking reptiles. At the end there was a hollow place scooped out of a wall, like a cupboard, and it was here that I found myself in close confinement. But the sight of all this was pleasant by comparison with what I felt there. What I have said is in no way an exaggeration.

*My feelings, I think, could not possibly be exaggerated, nor can anyone understand them. I felt a fire within my soul the nature of which I am utterly incapable of describing. My bodily sufferings were so intolerable that, though in my life I have endured the severest sufferings of this kind—the worst it is possible to endure, the doctors say, such as the shrinking of the nerves during my **paralysis** and many and **divers** more, some of them, as I have said, caused by the devil—none of them is of the smallest account by comparison with what I felt then, to say nothing of the knowledge that they would be endless and never-ceasing. And even these are nothing by comparison with the agony of my soul, an **oppression**, a **suffocation** and*

Ecstasy of St. Teresa

One of Teresa's most famous visions was portrayed by the Italian artist Gian Bernini in the painting *Ecstasy of St. Teresa.* It depicts her description, in *Life,* of an angel piercing her heart with the burning tip of a lance (long, spearlike weapon). Teresa wrote:

The pain was so great that it made me moan over and over, and the sweet delight into which that pain threw me was so intense that one could not want it to stop, or the soul be contented with anything but God. It is not bodily pain, but spiritual, though the body does not cease to share in it somewhat—and even very much so.

Paralysis: Loss of ability to move.

Divers: Various.

Oppression: A sense of being weighed down in body or mind.

Suffocation: Lack of air.

an **affliction** so deeply felt, and accompanied by such hopeless and distressing misery, that I cannot too forcibly describe it. To say that it is as if the soul were continually being torn from the body is very little, for that would mean that one's life was being taken by another; whereas in this case it is the soul itself that is tearing itself to pieces. The fact is that I cannot find words to describe that interior fire and that despair, which is greater than the most **grievous** tortures and pains. I could not see who was the cause of them, but I felt, I think, as if I were being both burned and **dismembered;** and I repeat that that interior fire and despair are the worst things of all.

In that **pestilential** spot, where I was quite powerless to hope for comfort, it was impossible to sit or lie, for there was no room to do so. I had been put in this place which looked like a hole in the wall, and those very walls, so terrible to the sight, bore down upon me and completely **stifled** me. There was no light and everything was in the blackest darkness. I do not understand how this can be, but, although there was no light, it was possible to see everything the sight of which can cause affliction. At that time it was not the Lord's will that I should see more of hell itself, but I have since seen another vision of frightful things, which are the punishment of certain **vices.** To look at, they seemed to me much more dreadful; but as I felt no pain, they caused me less fear. In the earlier vision the Lord was pleased that I should really feel those torments and that affliction of spirit, just as if my body had been suffering them. I do not know how it was, but I realized quite clearly that it was a great favour and that it was the Lord's will that I should see with my own eyes the place from which His mercy had delivered me. It is nothing to read a description of it, to think of different kinds of torture (as I have sometimes done, though rarely, as my soul made little progress by the road of fear): of how the devils tear the flesh with their **pincers** or of the various other tortures that I have read about—none of these are anything by comparison with this affliction, which is quite another matter. In fact, it is like a picture set against reality, and any burning on earth is a small matter compared with that fire.

I was terrified by all this, and, though it happened nearly six years ago, I still am as I write: even as I sit here, fear seems to be depriving my body of its natural warmth. I never recall any time when I have been suffering trials or pains and when everything that we can suffer on earth has seemed to me of the slightest importance by comparison with this; so, in a way, I think we complain without reason. I repeat, then, that this vision was one of the most **signal** favours which the Lord has **bestowed** upon me: it has been of the greatest benefit to

Affliction: Great suffering.

Grievous: Causing great pain or suffering.

Dismembered: Torn into pieces.

Pestilential: Deeply destructive.

Stifled: Smothered.

Vices: Moral faults.

Pincers: Claws.

Signal: Distinctive.

Bestowed: Granted as a gift.

me, both in taking from me all fear of the **tribulations** and disappointments of this life and also in strengthening me to suffer them and to give thanks to the Lord, Who, as I now believe, has delivered me from such terrible and never-ending torments.

Since that time, as I say, everything has seemed light to me by comparison with a single suffering as I had to bear during that vision. I am shocked at myself when I think that, after having so often read books which give some idea of the pains of hell, I was neither afraid of them nor rated them at what they are. What could I have been thinking of? How could anything give me satisfaction which was driving me to so awful a place? Blessed be Thou, my God, for ever! How plain it has become that Thou didst love me, much more than I love myself! How often, Lord, didst Thou deliver me from that gloomy prison and how I would make straight for it again, in face of Thy will!

This vision, too, was the cause of the very deep distress which I experience because of the great number of souls who are bringing damnation upon themselves—especially of those Lutherans, for they were made members of the Church through **baptism.** It also inspired me with **fervent** impulses for the good of souls: for I really believe that, to deliver a single one of them from such dreadful tortures, I would willingly die many deaths. After all, if we see anyone on earth who is especially dear to us suffering great trial or pain, our very nature seems to move us to **compassion,** and if his sufferings are severe they oppress us too. Who, then, could bear to look upon a soul's endless sufferings in that most terrible trial of all? No heart could possibly endure it without great affliction. For even earthly suffering, which after all, as we know, has a limit and will end with death, moves us to deep compassion. And that other suffering has no limit: I do not know how we can look on so calmly and see the devil carrying off as many souls as he does daily.

A detail of Gian Bernini's famous painting titled **Ecstasy of Saint Teresa.** ©Bettmann/Corbis. Reproduced by permission of Corbis Corporation.

Tribulations: Distressing experiences.

Baptism: Christian ritual in which a person is anointed with water and admitted into the Christian community.

Fervent: Intense.

Compassion: Sympathy with the distress of others.

What happened next...

Teresa's visions of hell influenced her work as a reformer. In 1560, two years before completing the first version of *Life,* she had made a decision to reform the Carmelites. She had long been troubled by the lax standards at the Convent of the Encarnacion, and she wanted to return the Carmelites to strict observance of the original rules of the order. After much opposition and struggle, in 1562 Pope Pius IV granted her permission to start the San Jose Convent for the Reformed Discalced Carmelite Order. Four nuns were transferred from the Convent of the Encarnacion to Teresa's convent. Next, four novices (probationary members of a religious community) joined the order against opposition from members of the church and the city of San Jose. This was the beginning of extensive reform efforts led by Teresa. She was instrumental in reforming not only the Carmelite convents for women but also the Carmelite monasteries for men. She was assisted in this goal by the Carmelite monk John of the Cross (1542–1591), who is also revered as a great mystical writer. Teresa spent the remainder of her life writing and traveling for the Reformed Discalced Carmelite Order. She produced numerous books, which are now considered classics in mystical literature. In addition to *Life,* these works include *Way of Perfection* (1564), *Meditations on the Song of Songs* (1566), *Spiritual Challenge* (1572), and *The Interior Castle* (1577).

There were several accounts of Teresa's last days before her death on October 4, 1582. According to one observer, she was kidnapped by Friar Antonio de Jesus Heredia to go to Alba to be present at the birth of an heir of the duke and duchess of Alba. Another account reported that Heredia ordered Teresa to go to Alba and she went willingly, even though she was ill. After arriving in Alba, she went to the convent, where she suffered a hemorrhage (uncontrolled bleeding) and was taken to the infirmary. Teresa knew she was dying, but she was joyful at the end. Witnesses said that a sweet fragrance filled the room at the time of her death. She was buried at the convent chapel in Alba, although many of her friends protested that she should be buried in Ávila. Her tomb is said to have emitted the same sweet fragrance and miracles were reported. Teresa was canonized (declared a saint, or one who is holy) in 1622, and in 1970 she was the first woman to be named a doctor of the church (one who defends Roman Catholic teachings).

Did you know...

- On at least six occasions Teresa was denounced before the Inquisition for unconventional beliefs and irregular religious practices. She was never formally tried for heresy, however.

- Nine months after Teresa died, Gracian, a Reformed Carmelite superior (head of a monastery), had her body exhumed, or removed from the grave. Although her robes were rotting, her body was well preserved. Gracian cut off her left hand and took it back to Ávila. He cut off one finger to use as a talisman (good luck charm), then reburied her in the tomb. Three years later, Gracian convinced the order of the Discalced to again exhume her body and take it to Ávila. Teresa's body was still preserved. The Discalceds considered this a supernatural occurrence since she had not been embalmed, or preserved with special fluids after death. They agreed to leave one arm in Alba to console the nuns there. By the eighteenth century, her body had been exhumed many times for examination and, little by little, body parts, bones, and pieces of flesh became missing.

For More Information

Books

Medwick, Cathleen. *Teresa of Ávila: the Progress of a Soul.* New York: Alfred A. Knopf, 1999.

Teresa de Ávila. *The Life of Teresa of Jesus.* Translated by E. Allison Peers. New York: Doubleday, 1960.

Web Sites

Knight, Kevin. "St. Teresa of Ávila." *Catholic Encyclopedia.* [Online] Available http://www.newadvent.org/cathen/14515b.htm, April 10, 2002.

St. Teresa of Ávila. *Way of Perfection.* Translated and edited by E. Allison Peers. [Online] Available http://www.ccel.org/t/teresa/way/main.html, April 10, 2002.

Teresa of Ávila. [Online] Available http://www.karmel.at/eng/teresa.htm, April 10, 2002.

Roman Catholic Church

"Profession of the Tridentine Faith" (1564)
Reprinted in *Confessions and Catechisms of the Reformation*
Edited by Mark A. Noll
Published in 1997

The Catholic Reformation was a reform movement that took place within the Roman Catholic Church from the mid-sixteenth century into the early seventeenth century. Reforms were initiated by the Council of Trent, a conference of church officials, in a series of reports titled *Canons and Decrees of the Council Trent.* (A canon is a church law. A decree is an official order that implements a canon.) The council met in twenty-seven sessions between 1545 and 1563. The Catholic Reformation is also known as the Counter Reformation, but some historians prefer not to use this term because it suggests that changes came as a reaction to the Protestant Reformation. The Protestant Reformation was a reform movement that began within the Catholic Church in the early 1500s and resulted in the establishment of Protestantism as a separate Christian faith. These historians note that Catholics were aware of the need for reform long before Protestants came on the scene.

Catholics seek reform

By the mid-1400s popes (supreme heads of the church), cardinals (church officials ranking directly below the pope), bishops (heads of church districts), and priests (pastors of congregations) had become greedy and corrupt. Neglecting their responsibilities as spiritual leaders, they pursued their own personal advancement and pleasure. Nepotism (appointing family members to church positions) and simony (selling of church offices) were common practices, and clergy of all ranks were noted for their luxurious lifestyles. In fact, the Catholic Church had more property and wealth than kings and princes. Clergymen routinely ignored celibacy rules (church prohibitions against having sexual relations) by keeping mistresses and fathering children. Other problems were equally serious. Bishops did not reside in their dioceses, or church districts, and priests did not live in their parishes as they were required to do. Bishops failed to supervise priests, who were often poorly educated and could not fulfill their duties to parishioners. Church doctrines, or teachings, had become empty rituals that were secondary to the quest for power. Even worse, clergymen misused their power to control and exploit church members.

Many Catholics were troubled by this situation. Outside the church, the *Devotio Moderna* (Modern Devotion) stressed a renewed commitment to spirituality. Christian humanist scholars also promoted an upright and devout life. (Humanists were scholars who promoted a human-centered literary and intellectual movement based on the revival of classical culture.) Within the church, Benedictine monks formed monasteries directly based on Christian teachings. Several priests openly criticized church officials' unethical practices and abuse of power. Among them was Girolamo Savonarola (1452–1498) of Florence, Italy, who achieved fame as an inspiring preacher. He was executed, however, because he challenged the pope's authority. Twenty years after Savonarola's death, the rapid rise of Protestantism brought more demands for reform. In keeping with a practice dating back to early times, many Catholics wanted to hold a general council of bishops to discuss problems. A general council met at Rome from 1515 until 1517. This gathering, called the Fifth Lateran Council, agreed to make various reforms. It adjourned shortly before the German reformer **Martin Luther** (see entry) posted his Ninety-Five Theses, a list of grievances against the church, at Wittenberg, Germany, in 1517. Luther attacked the practice of selling indulgences (partial forgive-

Pope Paul III was the first pope to show a serious interest in reforming the Roman Catholic Church. He appointed a committee of cardinals, known as the Council of Trent, to study problems within the church. *Photograph courtesy of The Library of Congress.*

ness of sins), but soon other reformers such as the Swiss priest **Huldrych Zwingli** (see entry) were questioning most of the teachings and practices of the Catholic Church. Popes showed no serious interest in reform until 1537, when Pope Paul III (1468–1549; reigned 1534–49) appointed a committee of cardinals to study problems in the church. Their report, *A Council ... for Reforming the Church,* denounced evils and abuses at all levels. Most of these abuses were laid at the door of the papacy (office of the pope) itself.

Council of Trent addresses problems

For the next few years Paul III tried to convene a council, but it had to be postponed several times, mainly because bishops felt threatened by his efforts to bring change. He therefore initiated his own reforms, such as encouraging new religious communities. Among them was the Society of Jesus (known as the Jesuits), an order for men founded by **Ignatius of Loyola** (see entry), which the pope approved in 1540. Two years later Paul III established an official church court, the Congregation of the Roman Inquisition, which was responsible for seeking out heretics (those who violate the laws of God and the church) and putting them on trial. In 1545 the pope finally succeeded in organizing the first session of the Council of Trent. He adjourned the council in 1547, however, because of poor attendance, an outbreak of typhus (bacterial disease), and a bad climate. The second session of Trent met in 1551 and 1552 under Pope Julius III (1487–1555; reigned 1550–55). The next pope, Marcellus II (1501–1555; reigned April–May 1555), held office only briefly and did not call any meetings. His successor, Paul IV (1476–1559; reigned 1555–59), opposed the council as a threat to papal authority and refused to hold meetings. He undertook his own reforms, strengthening the Roman Inquisition and establishing the Index of Prohibited Books, a list of "unholy and dangerous works." The final session of the Council of Trent met in 1562 and 1563, during the reign of Pope Pius IV (1499–1565; reigned 1559–65).

In 1564 Pope Pius IV released the Profession of the Tridentine Faith, which was a binding creed, or statement of faith, for teachers of church doctrines. It was a summary of the major decisions of the Council of Trent as reported in *Canons and Decrees.* Although no Protestants were mentioned by name in these documents, Protestant teachings were discussed by the council. The Profession of the Tridentine Faith therefore reflected the church's response to the main points of contention between Catholics and Protestants. The title was taken from *Tridentum,* the Latin word for Trent. The Profession of the Tridentine Faith is also known as the "Creed of Pius IV" and "The Creed of the Council of Trent."

The title page of the Vulgate Bible. The Council of Trent agreed that this version of the Bible should be the official Bible of the Catholic Church. *Reproduced by permission of Mary Evans Picture Library.*

Things to Remember While Reading "Profession of the Tridentine Faith":

- Paragraph one states that the Nicene Creed is the foundation of the Catholic faith. This position was declared by the Council of Trent in 1547. The Nicene Creed was written by early church fathers and adopted at the Council at Nicaea in C.E. 325.

- Paragraph three affirms that the ancient traditions of the church are equal to the truth of the Bible (the Christian holy book). Luther had asserted that the Bible, not the opinions of church officials, should be "the sole rule of faith." The delegates at Trent also agreed to accept the Vulgate (Latin translation) as the official Bible of the Catholic Church. This version of the Bible had been challenged by Luther and other Protestants as not being the true word of God.

- Paragraph four asserts that there are the seven sacraments, or holy rites rituals. Most Protestants rejected all sacraments except baptism and communion.

- Although paragraph five is brief, it addresses one of the major differences between Catholics and Protestants. Like Catholics, Protestants believed that humans are born with a sinful nature, called original sin. Protestants contended, however, that salvation, or the forgiveness of sins, is a gift from God, called grace. People are incapable of fulfilling God's will without grace, and the only way they can gain justification of God's grace is through faith, not good works. The Council of Trent reinforced the opposite view taken by Catholics, that people are capable of performing naturally good works through which they can earn grace. Nevertheless, they must be open to God's offer of grace, which enables them to fulfill his law. If they reject grace, they will not gain salvation.

- Paragraphs six and seven declare that Jesus of Nazareth (called the Christ; the founder of Christianity) is really and physically present in communion (known as the Eucharist). Communion is a ceremony, celebrated in a service called a mass, in which one receives bread and wine from a priest. According to Catholic belief, the bread becomes the body of Christ and the wine becomes his blood. Most Protestants rejected this belief, saying that the bread and wine are merely symbolic and do not actually become Christ's body and blood.

- Paragraph eight addresses other areas of conflict between Catholics and Protestants. First it asserts the Catholic belief in the existence of purgatory (a place between heaven and hell where a soul awaits forgiveness of sins), which was rejected by Protestants. Next it defends the veneration, or worship, of saints (people declared holy by the Catholic Church) and the practice of asking them for help and favors. Protestants thought Christians could learn such qualities as humility, faith, and hope from the lives of the saints, but they believed in praying directly to God. This paragraph also upholds the veneration of relics, or holy objects. Protestants declared such items as pieces of the "True Cross" on which Jesus of Nazareth was supposedly crucified, or locks of Jesus' baby hair, to be "fake."

- Paragraph nine states that pictures and statues of Christ, his mother Mary ("the perpetual virgin mother of God"), and other saints enhance the worship service. Protestants believed that such images only encouraged idolatry (worship of images, or false gods), so they should be removed from churches. This paragraph also defends the concept that Christ left an excess amount of God's grace when he died, and that people can gain some of this grace by purchasing indulgences. The sale of indulgences was attacked first by Luther and then by other Protestant reformers, who claimed this was simply a way for the church to get rich from people's weaknesses.

- Paragraph ten confirms that the pope ("bishop of Rome") is a direct descendent of Saint Peter (the first leader of Christianity after Jesus' death) and the vicar, or representative, of Jesus on Earth. Protestants rejected this belief, contending that no human being can claim such power, which belongs only to God.

- Paragraph eleven declares the decisions of the Council of Trent to be the only true teachings of Christianity. This means that anyone who does not accept the teachings is a heretic.

"Profession of the Tridentine Faith"

I. I,_____ , with a firm faith believe and profess all and every one of the things contained in that creed which the holy Roman Church makes use of:

"I believe in one God, the Father almighty; Maker of heaven and earth, and of all things visible and invisible.

"And in one Lord Jesus Christ, the only-begotten Son of God, begotten of the Father before all worlds [God of God], Light of Light, very God of very God, begotten, not made, being of one **substance** with the Father; by whom all things were made; who, for us men and for our salvation, came down from heaven, and was **incarnate** by the **Holy Ghost** of the virgin Mary, and was made man; and was crucified also for us under **Pontius Pilate;** he suffered and was

Substance: Essence.

Incarnate: In bodily form.

Holy Ghost: Holy Spirit; third person of the Holy Trinity (God the Father, Son, and Holy Spirit).

Pontius Pilate: Roman official who condemned Jesus to death.

Quick: Living.

Prophets: Writers of the books of the Old Testament, the first part of the Bible.

Apostolic: Relating to the teachings of the New Testament, the second part of the Bible.

Baptism: Christian sacrament marked by the use of water and admitting the recipient into the Christian community.

Resurrection: Rising.

Steadfastly: Firm in belief.

Ecclesiastic: Pertaining to the church.

To wit: Specifically.

Confirmation: Conferring the gift of the Holy Spirit.

Penance: Act of showing sorrow for a sin.

Extreme unction: Sacrament in which a priest anoints an prays for the recovery and salvation of a critically ill or injured person.

Holy orders: Confirmation of those who administer the sacraments.

Matrimony: Marriage.

Reiterated: Repeated.

Sacrilege: Violation of what is consecrated (made holy) by god.

Aforesaid: Previously stated.

Propitiatory: Gaining of favor of good will.

buried; and the third day he rose again, according to the Scriptures; and ascended into heaven, and sitteth on the right hand of the Father; and he shall come again, with glory, to judge both the **quick** and the dead; whose kingdom shall have no end.

"And [I believe] in the Holy Ghost, the Lord and Giver of life; who proceedeth from the Father [and the Son]; who with the Father and the Son together is worshiped and glorified; who spake by the **Prophets.** And [I believe] one holy catholic and **apostolic** church. I acknowledge one **baptism** for the baptism of sins; and I look for the **resurrection** of the dead, and the life of the world to come. Amen."

II. I most **steadfastly** admit and embrace apostolic and **ecclesiastic** traditions, and all other observances and constitutions of the same church.

III. I also admit the holy Scriptures, according to that sense which our holy mother Church has held and does hold, to which it belongs to judge of the true sense and interpretation of the Scriptures; neither will I ever take and interpret them otherwise than according to the unanimous consent of the fathers.

IV. I also profess that there are truly and properly seven sacraments of the new law, instituted by Jesus Christ our Lord, and necessary for the salvation of mankind, although not all for every one, **to wit:** baptism, **confirmation,** the Eucharist, **penance, extreme unction, holy orders,** and **matrimony;** and that they confer grace; and that of these, baptism, confirmation, and ordination cannot be **reiterated** without **sacrilege.** I also receive and admit the received and approved ceremonies of the Catholic Church, used in the solemn administration of the **aforesaid** sacraments.

V. I embrace and receive all and every one of the things which have been defined and declared in the holy Council of Trent concerning original sin and justification.

VI. I profess, likewise, that in the Mass there is offered to God a true, proper, and **propitiatory** sacrifice for the living and the dead; and that in the most holy sacrament of the Eucharist there is truly, really, and substantially, the body and blood, together with the soul and divinity of our Lord Jesus Christ; and that there is made a change of the whole essence of the bread into the body, and of the whole essence of the wine into the blood; which change the Catholic Church calls transubstantiation.

VII. I also confess that under either kind alone Christ is received whole and entire, and a true sacrament.

VIII. I firmly hold that there is a purgatory, and that the souls therein detained are helped by the **suffrages** of the faithful. Likewise, that the saints reigning with Christ are to be honored and **invoked,** and that they offer up prayers to God for us, and that their relics are to be had in veneration.

IX. I most firmly assert that the images of Christ, and of the perpetual virgin the mother of God, and also of the other saints, ought to be had and retained, and that due honor and veneration are to be given them. I also affirm that the power of indulgences was left by Christ in the church, and that the use of them is most wholesome to Christian people.

X. I acknowledge the holy Catholic Apostolic Roman Church for the mother and mistress of all churches; and I promise and swear true obedience to the bishop of Rome, successor to Saint Peter, prince of the apostles, and vicar of Jesus Christ.

XI. I likewise undoubtingly receive and profess all other things delivered, defined, and declared by the sacred canons and general councils, and particularly by the holy Council of Trent; and I condemn, reject, and **anathematize** all things contrary thereto, and all heresies which the church has condemned, rejected, and anathematized.

XII. I do, at this present, freely profess and truly hold this true Catholic faith, without which no one can be saved; and I promise most constantly to retain and confess the same entire and inviolate, with God's assistance, to the end of my life. And I will take care, as far as in me lies, that it shall be held, taught, and preached by my subjects, or by those the care of whom shall **appertain** to me in my office. This I promise, vow, and swear—so help me God, and these holy **Gospels** of God.

What happened next...

The Council of Trent brought about positive changes. Foremost was the clarification of church doctrines, which had previously been confusing for many Catholics. Popes, councils, and theologians had said different things at different times about purgatory, the sacraments, the veneration of saints, indulgences, and communion, among other church

Suffrages: Short prayers in behalf of someone.

Invoked: Appealed to for help.

Anathematize: Cursed by the church.

Appertain: Belong or relate to.

Gospels: Message of Christ, kingdom of God, and salvation.

The Council of Trent met from 1545 to 1569. The council brought about positive changes within the Roman Catholic Church.
©Archivo Iconografico, S. A./Corbis. Reproduced by permission of Corbis Corporation.

teachings. After the Council of Trent these doctrines became perfectly clear, to both Catholics and Protestants. Acknowledging that corruption was a serious problem, the council issued strong rulings for eliminating unethical and illegal practices. Pope Pius implemented these changes by appointing reformers to high office. As a result, church officials could no longer engage in simony and nepotism. Bishops and priests had to live in their parishes, and bishops were ordered to enforce greater discipline over priests. Seminaries were established in each diocese for the education of priests. The pope was given more control over cardinals and bishops. In addition, artists painted masterpieces on religious subjects and musicians composed grand choral works based on sacred texts, introducing a new sense of spirituality into religious life. At the same time, however, the Roman Inquisition and the Index of Prohibited Books ruined the lives of many people.

Although abuses were not entirely eliminated, the decrees of the Council of Trent were generally successful. By the turn of the seventeenth century the Catholic Church seemed to have survived assaults from Protestants. Catholics and Protestants were even living together in harmony in some places. Yet this situation did not last. In 1618 Europe erupted into another round of religious disputes, which escalated into the Thirty Years' War (1618–48), now known as the first armed conflict to involve all major world powers. The Peace of Westphalia, the treaty signed after the Thirty Years' War, was a landmark in European history. The Protestant Reformation and the Catholic Reformation had come to an end. Religion no longer played an important role in issues that divided European states—a new map of Europe had been drawn according to the principles of religious freedom.

Did you know...

- The Nicene Creed was adopted as a statement of faith by many Protestant denominations.

- In 1555 Pope Paul IV strengthened the Roman Inquisition, which had been established by Paul III. At that time the church wrongly suspected Jews of influencing the Protestant Reformation, so Paul IV established the Jewish ghetto (a part of the city in which a minority group is forced to live) at Rome. He required all Jews to wear an identifying badge, thus separating them from Christians.

- In 1559 Paul IV issued the first edition of the Index of Prohibited Books. The list included the complete writings of such Protestant reformers as Martin Luther, Huldrych Zwingli, the French-born Swiss evangelist **John Calvin** (see entry), and Scottish Presbyterian leader John Knox. Also condemned were some works by the Dutch humanist Desiderius Erasmus, *The Prince* by the Italian political theorist **Niccolò Machiavelli** (see entry), and the Koran (the Islamic holy book). Appearing on later lists were such Renaissance classics as sonnets by the Italian poet Petrarch, poems by the Italian courtesan (woman who sells sexual favors to members of a court) Veronica Franco, *Book of the Courtier* by Italian author Baldassare Castiglione, and the scientific works of **Galileo** (see entry). The Index of Prohibited Books was terminated in 1948 with the publication of the twentieth and final edition.

In 1966 the Catholic Church abolished the Index and classified it as an historical document.

For More Information

Books

Noll, Mark A., ed. *Confessions and Catechisms of the Reformation.* Vancouver, B.C.: Regent College Publishing, 1997.

Web Sites

Halsall, Paul. "Council of Trent: Rules on Prohibited Books." *Modern History Sourcebook.* [Online] Available http://www.fordham.edu/halsall/mod/trent-booksrules.html, April 10, 2002.

"Paul III." *Infoplease.com.* [Online] Available http://www.infoplease.com/ce6/people/A0837895.html, April 10, 2002.

"Savonarola, Girolamo." *MSN Encarta.* [Online] Available http://encarta.msn.com/index/conciseindex/4B/04BA3000.htm?z=1&pg=2&br=1, April 10, 2002.

"Trent, Council of." *Infoplease.com.* [Online] Available http://www.infoplease.com/ce6/society/A0849364.html, April 10, 2002.

Witch-Hunts

6

During the Reformation period, witchcraft trials were held throughout Europe by officials of both the Roman Catholic Church and the newly emerging Protestant faiths. In 1484 Pope Innocent VIII issued an official order, called a papal bull, that ordered the eradication of witches and other heathens. Although many such documents had previously been released, the Papal Bull of 1484 was aided by the printing press, which rapidly spread information about so-called witches throughout Europe. The printing press also facilitated the mass publication of more than thirty scholarly works on witchcraft that were written during the fifteenth century. They were the basis of the most famous witchcraft study, *Malleus maleficarum* (Hammer of Witches). This work became the official handbook for witchcraft trials, which reached a peak in 1580s and continued into the mid-seventeenth century.

Heinrich Kramer and Jacob Sprenger

Excerpt from Malleus Maleficarum *(1486)*

Reprinted in *The Malleus Maleficarum of Heinrich Kramer and James Sprenger*

**Edited by Montague Summers
Published in 1971**

During the Reformation, in the sixteenth century, witch-craft trials were held throughout Europe by officials of both the Roman Catholic Church and the newly emerging Protestant faiths. The term "Reformation" originated with the movement to reform the Roman Catholic Church. Known as the Protestant Reformation, it was initiated in 1517 when the German priest **Martin Luther** (see entry) posted his "Nine-ty-Five Theses" in Wittenberg, Germany, to protest corrupt practices in the Catholic Church. Eventually, advocates of church reform, who were first called Lutherans and then came to be known as Protestants, separated from the church and organized their own religious groups. Almost simultane-ously the Catholic Church convened the Council of Trent and was launching reform efforts that became known as the Catholic Reformation or the Counter Reformation (see **Roman Catholic Church** entry). Part of the Catholic Re-formation was the Roman Inquisition, the continuation of a church court established in the thirteenth century to search out and punish heretics (those who violate the laws of God and the church). Although the Inquisition remained separate from the witch trials, it created an atmosphere of hysteria and suspicion that facilitated the targeting of supposed witches as heretics. Yet witch-hunts were by no means carried out solely by the Catholic Church. In fact, Protestants were equally active in hunting and punishing those who violated the strict codes of their new religious groups.

The purpose of the witch trials, specifically, was to discover and punish people who committed heresy by practicing harmful magic or worshiping the devil (also called Satan; the figure that represents evil). Harmful magic was the use of a supernatural or mysterious power that caused death, bodily injury, illness, or some other misfortune. According to thinking at the time, this type of magic, often called sorcery, could harm an entire community, such as when a witch brought down a hailstorm that destroyed crops. Worship of the devil involved not only the making of a face-to-face pact with the evil spirit but also group worship of him in secret ceremonies at night. During these ceremonies, known as sabbaths, witches supposedly ate children, danced naked, and had sexual intercourse with demons, or evil spirits. The word for witchcraft in most European languages could also mean white (beneficial) magic, but most trial judges considered this type of witchcraft to be a lesser offense and punished it less harshly.

Malleus fuels witch-hunts

The concept of witchcraft had gradually been developed over three centuries by theologians (religious scholars) and inquisitors (Inquisition judges). At its root was the Christian belief, first expressed by church fathers in the 1200s and 1300s, that the power of all magic came from the devil. Since magic arose from the devil, it was therefore a form of heresy. By the 1500s the formal charge of heresy was directed against people who were suspected of casting spells and committing evil deeds. Theologians and judges began to think of witches as members of a new and dangerous heretical sect (nonmainstream religious group). Their crimes included rejection of religion and morality, conspiracy (plots against the government), and magical destruction of life and property. Witchcraft had been added to the list of official punishable heresies in 1320, but it did not become a primary target for more than a century. Then in 1484 Pope Innocent VIII (1432–1492; reigned 1484–92) issued an edict, called a papal

An illustration of a witch, a demon, and a warlock (male witch) riding on brooms toward a peasant woman. The second part of *Malleus Maleficarum* described the satanic activities of witches such as these pictured here. *Reproduced by permission of Hulton Archive.*

bull, that ordered the eradication, or complete destruction, of witches and other heathens (those who do not acknowledge the God of the Bible). Although many such edicts had previously been issued, the Papal Bull of 1484 was aided by a recent invention, the printing press, which rapidly spread information about so-called witches throughout Europe.

The printing press also aided the mass publication of more than thirty scholarly works on witchcraft that were written during the fifteenth century. They were the basis of the most famous witchcraft study, *Malleus maleficarum* (Hammer of Witches), which became the second-best-selling book (the first was the Bible) in Europe for more than two centuries. This work was the official handbook for detecting, capturing, trying, and executing witches. It was written in 1486 by Austrian priest Heinrich Kramer (also Kraemer) and German priest Jakob (also James) Sprenger, at the request of Innocent VIII. As the main justification for persecution of witches, the authors relied on a brief passage in the Bible (the book of Exodus, chapter 22, verse 18), which states: "Thou shalt not suffer a witch to live." According to the *Malleus,* "it has never yet been known that an innocent person has been punished on suspicion of witch-craft and there is no doubt that god would never permit such a thing to happen...."

The following excerpt, from chapter two of *Malleus Maleficarum,* describes the three kinds of witches and how they used their powers.

Things to Remember While Reading an Excerpt from *Malleus Maleficarum:*

- The *Malleus Maleficarum* was a three-part work that described witchcraft in elaborate detail. The first part acknowledged the existence of witches and condemned them as demons and heretics. Much power was given to an accuser, regardless of his or her status in the community, and anyone accused of witchcraft was immediately discredited. The *Malleus* specified that even criminals, the insane, or children could testify against an accused witch once the person was brought to trial.

- The second part of the book described the satanic activities of witches. Special emphasis was placed on the relationship between female witches and the devil. Witches were accused of eating children, having sex with the devil, going to sabbaths with other witches and demons, and having evil connections with animals known as "familiars." Witches were considered the human agents of the devil and were held responsible for any number of imagined or real catastrophes.

- The third part of the *Malleus* outlined the legal procedures required for finding, trying, and executing witches. This section gave free license to lawyers and clergymen, enabling them to take any means necessary to obtain a signed or verbal confession. To protect lawyers and clergy themselves from charges of murder, all accused witches were presumed guilty and their innocence did not have to be proven. Any accused person could be taken from his or her home to the courts and subjected to various methods of extreme torture. The book prescribed these methods in detail, noting various markings that could "prove" a person was a witch. Such "evidence" included, warts, excessive body hair, or extra nipples—all of which gave reason for intense punishment.

Excerpt from Malleus Maleficarum

*The method by which they profess their **sacrilege** through an open **pact** of **fidelity** to devils varies according to the several practices to which different witches are **addicted.** And to understand this it first must be noted that there are, as was shown in The First Part of the **treatise,** three kinds of witches; namely, those who injure but cannot cure; those who cure but, through some strange pact with the devil, cannot injure; and those who both injure and cure. And among those who injure, one class in particular stands out, which can perform every sort of witchcraft and spell, **comprehending** all that all the others can individually can do. **Wherefore,** if we describe the method of profession in their case, it will **suffice** also for all the other kinds. And this class is made up of those who, against every instinct of human or animal nature, are in the habit of eating and **devouring** the children of their own species.*

*And this is the most powerful class of witches, who practise innumerable other harms also. For they raise hailstorms and hurtful **tempests** and lightnings; cause **sterility** in men and animals; offer to devils, or otherwise kill, the children whom they do not devour. But these are only the children who have not been re-born by **baptism** at the **font,** for they cannot devour those who have been baptized, nor any without God's permission. They can also, before the eyes of their parents, and when no one is in sight, throw into the water children walking by the water side; they make horses go mad under their riders; they can transport themselves from place to place through the air, wither in body or in imagination; they can affect Judges and **Magistrates** so that they cannot hurt them; they can cause themselves and others to keep silence under torture; they can bring about a great trembling in the hands and horror in the minds of those who would arrest them; they can show to others **occult** things and future events, by the information of devils, though this may sometimes have a natural cause...; they can see absent things*

Sacrilege: An outrageous violation of God's laws or practices.

Pact: Contract.

Fidelity: Commitment.

Addicted: To have a compulsive need for something.

Treatise: A written study of a topic or issue.

Comprehending: Understanding.

Wherefore: An explanation or reason.

Suffice: To make do.

Devouring: To greedily eat or use up.

Tempests: Violent weather.

Sterility: Incapable of producing offspring.

Baptism: Symbolic practice used in religion where a person is absolved of their sins by use of water.

Font: A basin that holds holy water for baptisms.

Magistrates: Government officials similar to judges.

Occult: A faction of religion which relies on magic and mythology for its practices.

Two witches casting a spell over an open fire. The first part of *Malleus Maleficarum* describes the three types of witches. *Reproduced by permission of Archive Photos, Inc.*

as if they were present; they can turn the minds of men to **inordinate** love or hatred; they can at times strike whom they will with lightening and even kill some men and animals; they can make of no effect the **generative** desires, and even the powers of **copulation,** cause **abortion,** kill infants in the mother's **womb** by a **mere exterior** touch; they can at times **bewitch** men and animals with a mere look, without touching them, and cause death; they dedicate their own children to devils; and in short, as has been said, they can

Inordinate: Exceeding reasonable limits.

Generative: Having the power of reproducing.

Copulation: The joining of beings in sexual intercourse.

Abortion: Termination of pregnancy.

Womb: Uterus; the place where babies form and develop inside the mother until they are born.

Mere: Small part or segment.

Exterior: Outside.

Bewitch: To cast a spell over.

*cause all the **plagues** which other witches can only cause in part, that is, when the Justice of God permits such things to be. All these things this most powerful of all classes of witches can do, but they cannot undo them.*

What happened next...

The *Malleus* became the guide for civil and church law, going through twenty-eight editions between 1486 and 1600. It was accepted by Roman Catholics and Protestants alike. The most important impact of *Malleus* was that it united the church and the state, making torture legal as a means of obtaining confessions from accused witches. These methods were extremely efficient. Thousands gave in, no matter how false or ridiculous the charges might have seemed, to save themselves from additional torture. In turn, the confessions fanned mass hysteria, proving that the initial suspicions had been correct and creating an enemy out of innocent people. Officials in some regions used so-called tests that pointed to the guilt of an accused person in various ways. A popular method in England (where torture was considered a crime) was the water test. The results were supposed to determine whether or not a person was indeed a witch—yet nobody could actually pass the test. It involved tying the accused person's arms and legs together, then throwing him or her into a body of water. If the victim sank, he or she was not a witch. Since multilayered clothing was worn at the time, people quite often ended up floating because their clothes created pockets of air that forced them to remain at the surface of the water. Many accused witches were declared guilty by this method, then publicly burned at a stake in the center of town. Burning was considered another test, as well as the most severe form of punishment: it was thought that witches could survive fire because of their association with the devil. The prevalence of the fire test led to this era being called "The Burning Times."

Witchcraft prosecutions reached a peak between 1580 and 1660, and officially ended on June 17, 1782, when

Plagues: Disaster or disease.

the last execution was held in Switzerland. Trials took place mainly in France, Germany, and Switzerland, but also extended throughout Western Europe, into pockets of northern and eastern Europe. The witch craze eventually spread to the American colonies, where the famous witch trials began in Salem, Massachusetts, in 1693. Spain was one of the few countries not associated with the witch-hunts because Spanish officials did not believe in witchcraft as defined by the *Malleus*. In Spain suspected witches were locked up in convents (houses for women who are dedicated to religious life). It is difficult to establish the number of people who were killed in the antiwitch campaign because many died in jails from torture and starvation and were not recorded in official execution counts. Most estimates state that one hundred thousand trials were held and that about half of the trials resulted in executions. On average, 80 percent of the accused were women and 85 percent of those actually executed were women. Most men who were accused were either related to women who had been tried, or they had criminal records implicating them in other crimes against the church and state. Nearly all of the accused were poor or came from the lower classes.

Although there were some vocal opponents of the witchcraft trials, very few survived their own outspokenness. Most were considered guilty by association and were virtually powerless against the campaign. By the end of the seventeenth century, however, two factors brought the persecutions to a halt. First, officials were running out of victims: so many people had been killed that entire regional populations had been altered. The high number of executions began raising concerns about the need to slow down. In response to atrocities in Germany, Holy Roman Emperor Ferdinand II (1578–1637; ruled 1619–37) issued a decree to stop the killings. Other officials slowed down the witch-hunt as they began to realize it was no longer necessary. Another factor that helped grind the machine to a halt was a new European ideology, which envisioned a more rational and ordered universe. This shift in thinking eventually led to the era called the Enlightenment that began in the eighteenth century. By then past history was dismissed as having been the result of ancient, irrational superstitions.

Did you know...

- Before the onset of the witch trials in the Reformation period, Jews were especially vulnerable to charges of heresy, as were Muslims (followers of the Islamic religion), homosexuals, and Gypsies (wandering people who originated in India). Many of the same accusations that later fueled the witch-hunts were initially aimed at these peoples. For example, the word "synagogue" (a Jewish house of worship) was redefined to describe a time and place of devil worship. The word "sabbath," traditionally associated with the Jewish day of rest, came to symbolize large group meetings between witches and the devil. Even the stereotyped appearance of a witch was borrowed from the racist caricature (distorted representation of certain physical features) of Jews and Arabs as having extremely large, crooked noses.

- One of the most common means of torture was the stretching rack, a device that would slowly tear a person limb from limb as he or she was repeatedly commanded to confess to specific crimes. A similar tool was the strapado, which involved attaching weights to a victim's legs, then slowly lifting the person off the ground so that the legs would begin to tear away from the body. Another method involved the victim being stripped naked and slowly cut in half by being dragged along a very tight rope. Some people were tied to stakes and placed near a fire that would slowly "cook" them. Many others had their eyes gouged out or were beaten, raped, disemboweled (internal organs cut out), dropped from high above the ground, or subjected to numerous devices created specially for the task. Also popular were "Spanish boots," devices that were put on a victim's legs and could work in either of two ways. One used internal vices that would slowly crush the victim's legs, while the other involved pouring boiling water or oil into the "boots."

- Relatives of accused witches were charged money for all manner of details involved in a trial. Not only did they pay the salary of the judge, they also bore the cost of food and lodging for the accused in prison. In addition, relatives were charged for the wood and straw used for kindling the execution fire, and they were billed for the lavish banquets typically held for officials before mass executions. In the case of accused people who had no relatives in the region, personal property was confiscated to pay the bills. The result was that many people lost their land, money, and lives while a few witch-hunters and judges accumulated wealth with every successful trial.

For More Information

Books

Barstow, Anne Llewellyn. *Witchcraze: A New History of the European Witch Hunts*. San Francisco: Harper, 1999.

Summers, Montague, ed. *The Malleus Maleficarum of Heinrich Kramer and James Sprenger*. New York: Dover Publications, 1971.

Web Sites

Early Modern Europe: The Witch Hunts. [Online] Available http://history. hanover.edu/early/wh.html, April 10, 2002.

Pavlac, Brian A. *Women and European Witch Hunts*. [Online] Available http://www.kings.edu/womens_history/witch.html, April 10, 2002.

Index

Bold type indicates main entries and their page numbers. Illustrations are marked by (ill.)